Burgess Sport Teaching Series

TEACHING VOLLEYBALL

Richard H. Cox
Kansas State University

Burgess Publishing Company
Minneapolis, Minnesota

Consulting Editor: Robert D. Clayton, Colorado State University

Editorial: Wayne Schotanus, Marta Reynolds, Elisabeth Sövik
Art: Joan Gordon, Lynn Dwyer, Adelaide Trettel
Production: Morris Lundin, Pat Barnes
Composition: Terry Purcell

Cover Design: Adelaide Trettel

Burgess Publishing Company
7108 Ohms Lane
Minneapolis, Minnesota 55435

Contents

Acknowledgments

I am indebted to a host of people who have contributed to the completion of this work. First of all to Dr. Robert Clayton for reading the entire manuscript and for making countless and invaluable suggestions. Second, to Gary Horacek and Bernard Felton for the photographic work, and to Susan Haas, Susie Long, Gabriel Castro, and Lacy McMullen for serving as photographic subjects. Next, to Bill Schroeder for the many hours he contributed to complete the artwork. And, finally, to my wife, Linda, who faithfully typed the entire manuscript . . . twice.

1

Introduction

This book was written for the individual who is or who will be a volleyball teacher or coach. Although the concepts and techniques described for teaching and coaching volleyball are most applicable to the professional in the public schools, it is expected that professionals in commercial or social-service (YMCA-YWCA) positions will also find the material useful.

In my opinion, a book on how to *teach* volleyball as opposed to how to *play* it is greatly needed. In writing this book, I have tried to place myself in the position of the neophyte teacher and consider the many questions that must be asked daily. For example: What skills should be taught in a beginning class? What are the basic problems that beginners have in learning a new skill? Are there teaching tips that can speed up learning? What kind of volleyballs should be selected? How important are nets and standards to quality instruction? Does age or skill level make any difference in the method of instruction? Can a successful teacher also be a successful coach? Is coaching really a lot different from teaching?

It has been the practice over the last few years to make a distinction between teaching the concepts of physical education and coaching a group of athletes. Throughout this book, an effort has been made to remove these artificial differences and to view the coach as a specialized teacher. The contents this of this book, therefore, can generally be applied to both coaching and teaching. It may be that the student preparing to be a teacher may not be interested in those few chapters alluding specifically to coaching. Conversely, if this book were adopted for a volleyball coaching class, students might not need to study intently those chapters dealing specifically with teaching.

To use this book effectively, students need to recognize that they must be actively involved in problem solving. While I have tried to provide structured guidance for every conceivable situation, it has not been my intent to write a "cookbook" for teaching volleyball. Rather, numerous examples and useful tips are given throughout to help students arrive at their own solutions in actual teacher-learning situations. The student projects suggested at the end of each chapter are also designed to help students broaden their practical knowledge of the sport and develop effective techniques for teaching.

2

The Performance Objective

In any kind of instructional situation, it is advisable that the teacher establish a set of learning objectives. A unit of instruction that has no particular goal has little chance of success. Even if the instructor does have some general expectations for desirable outcomes, if those outcomes are not specific, there will be no way of knowing whether they have been realized. In our age of accountability, the teacher and the student need to know what the objectives of a unit of instruction are and the specific criteria used for measuring their achievement.

Performance objectives (behavioral objectives) are specific statements of proposed educational outcomes. Popularized by Mager (1962), this sort of instructional objective has been strongly recommended for use by physical educators.

THE NATURE OF THE PERFORMANCE OBJECTIVE

Because it is observable, an instructional objective written as a performance objective is easy to measure. The performance objective will identify *specific* and *minimum* levels of acceptable performance and also the means for evaluating performances.

One of the keys to writing performance objectives is the use of direct, unambiguous language. For example, the nature of the verb object that is placed in the blank of the sentence, "The student will be able to_____," is of paramount importance. Certain verb objects such as "to understand" or "to appreciate" tend to make a performance objective ambiguous and unmeasurable. Infinitives (verb objects) such as "to identify" or "to perform" are less ambiguous and more measurable.

Outlined in Table 2.1 are three criteria for writing performance objectives and examples of properly and improperly stated performance objectives.

In row one of Table 2.1, it is clear that the improperly stated objective does not describe *specific observable performance.* What exactly does it mean *to be capable of playing volleyball?* This objective defies observation and measurement. In the properly stated objective, however, the performance is described in terms of observable behavior. In row two, the improperly stated objective uses the ambiguous term *efficiently.* How can you tell if the student has achieved an acceptable level of performance? The properly stated objective describes the *minimal acceptable level of performance* as 30 passes against a flat wall. Finally, in row three of the table, the improperly written objective does not clarify how the performance will be evaluated. Again, two ambiguous words, *correctly* and *reasonable,* are used; but the properly stated objective clearly establishes *how* forearm passing performance will be evaluated.

TABLE 2.1
CRITERIA FOR WRITING PERFORMANCE OBJECTIVES

CRITERIA	THE PERFORMANCE OBJECTIVE	
	Improperly Stated	**Properly Stated**
Describe the observable performance or behavior expected of the learner.	The learner will be capable of playing volleyball.	The learner will be able to forearm pass a volleyball.
Describe the minimum acceptable levels of performance or behavior.	The learner will be able to forearm pass efficiently.	The learner will be able to forearm pass a volleyball against a flat wall 30 times.
Describe the evaluative criteria to be used to determine acceptable performance.	The learner will be able to forearm pass a volleyball correctly against a flat wall a reasonable number of times.	The learner will be able to forearm pass a volleyball against a wall and above a horizontal line drawn 8 feet from the floor, 30 times in 60 seconds.

TAXONOMY OF PERFORMANCE OBJECTIVES

Traditionally, physical education objectives have been categorized into four basic areas: organic development, neuromuscular development, interpretive development, and impulsive development (Neilson and Bronson, 1965). In recent years physical educators have generally adopted the educational taxonomy developed by Bloom (1956). This taxonomy divided educational objectives into the cognitive domain, the psychomotor domain, and the affective domain. While this taxonomy has been useful to educators in general, it is somewhat lacking in terms of its ability to describe physical education objectives. Corbin (1976) points out this problem in an attempt to develop a more useful taxonomy for physical education. His taxonomy categorizes the objectives of physical education into five basic areas.

According to Corbin, physical education objectives can be divided into the physical fitness domain, the skill domain, the cognitive domain, the affective domain, and the personal-social domain. The Corbin approach, it should be pointed out, has been adopted for this book.

The Physical Fitness Domain

Aspects of physical fitness can be subdivided into *health-related* and *skill-related* aspects of fitness (Corbin, 1973). The health-related aspects include such items as endurance, flexibility, strength, and muscular endurance. Skill-related aspects include agility, reaction time, balance, coordination, and speed. The item of explosive power might be considered to be both health- and skill-related.

In teaching a course in volleyball, the instructor will be particularly interested in the development of *explosive power* of the legs for jumping, *strength* of the arms and hands for setting, and *agility* and *coordination* for blocking and spiking. Through proper application of the drills outlined in this text for skill acquisition, many of the physical fitness aspects listed above will be developed.

The Skill Domain

The development of skill in specific sport activities is of major concern in the skill domain. For example, in the game of volleyball the instructor is interested in the development of such skills as forearm passing, setting, spiking, blocking, and serving.

To assist the instructor in the development of skill, numerous drills are outlined in chapters 5, 6, and 7. Because development of skill is of prime concern, the teacher must make every effort to motivate students to practice the individual skills. This is best accomplished through the use of well-conceived learning experiences (drills and lead-up games).

The Cognitive Domain

The cognitive domain is concerned with knowledge, comprehension, application, analysis, synthesis, and evaluation. Learning in the cognitive domain generally begins with the acquisition of knowledge (i.e., the learning of the rules in volleyball). However, for the cognitive objective to be fully realized, the learner must do more than memorize a set of rules. The learner must be able to comprehend, apply, analyze, synthesize, and evaluate situations related to the rules of volleyball. This same line of reasoning applies to the fulfillment of cognitive-domain objectives for strategies of play, systems of defense and offense, and knowledge of skill techniques.

In achieving specific objectives in the cognitive domain, the teacher must provide opportunities for practical application. For example, the students could develop a greater understanding of the rules of volleyball if they were required to assist in officiating an intra-class tournament. In addition, they could volunteer to serve as linespersons in local interscholastic or collegiate volleyball matches.

The Affective Domain

Learning in the affective domain relates to our feelings, attitudes, values, and motives. Through physical education activities, the student has an opportunity to learn to be sensitive to the ideas and behaviors of others, to be responsive to the rules of the game, to develop a personal value system, and to incorporate sports participation into his or her personal philosophy of life.

Although physical educators have traditionally given a great deal of lip service to this particular learning domain, it is a rare teacher who truly knows whether or not students have actually developed in the affective domain. This is partly due to the failure to write *measurable* performance objectives. Teachers can most effectively assist their students in the development of affective considerations by composing meaningful performance objectives that will result in desirable affective outcomes.

The Personal-Social Domain

While the personal-social domain is affective in nature, it is classified separately here to account for certain personal adjustments that do not fit well into Bloom's (1956) three-part taxonomy. Physical education is a discipline in which positive social interaction and adjustment are possible. The development of such qualities as leadership, sportsmanship, and self-confidence results quite naturally from regular participation in sport and physical education.

Again, as in the affective domain, the *average* physical education teacher has little observable evidence to support the contention that physical education develops leadership, sportsmanship, or self-confidence, a fact that is attributed to the failure to write specific *measurable* performance objectives.

SAMPLE PERFORMANCE OBJECTIVES

The following are sample performance objectives from all five learning domains. They are specifically for high school girls completing a course in beginning volleyball, but with slight modifications they can be made applicable to other age groups and to boys as well as girls (see chapter 8, Evaluation).

Physical Fitness Domain Objectives

As an end result of a six-week unit on volleyball, the learners will be able to:
1. Jump 14 inches vertically off the floor without using an approach of arm swing.
2. Do 10 properly (according to specifications) executed burpees in 20 seconds.
3. Do the AAHPER shuttle run test in under 10.8 seconds.
4. Run-walk 1900 yards in 12 minutes.

Skill Domain Objectives

As an end result of a six-week unit on volleyball, the learner will be able to:
1. Forearm pass a volleyball against a flat wall and above a horizontal line drawn eight feet from the floor 20 times in 60 seconds (Brumbach test).
2. Face pass a volleyball against a flat wall, above a horizontal line drawn 11 feet from the floor and between two vertical line markers set five feet apart, 20 times in 60 seconds (AAHPER volley test).
3. Earn a score of 20 on the AAHPER volleyball serving test.
4. Jump in the air, hit a volleyball downward hard enough for it to rebound from the floor to a wall and back behind a 15-foot restraining line 8 times in 60 seconds (Stanley spike test).

Cognitive Domain Objectives

At the completion of a six-week unit of volleyball, the learner will be able to:
1. Earn a score of 70 percent correct responses on a written examination that tests the student's understanding of the rules of the game of volleyball.
2. Demonstrate knowledge and understanding of the 3-deep defense in volleyball by diagramming positions and listing responsibilities of each defensive player.
3. List and describe three mechanical principles involved in executing the forearm pass for service reception.
4. State where and by whom the game of volleyball was invented.
5. Indicate the court dimensions and net heights for the men's game and the women's game.

Affective Domain Objectives

As a result of participation in a unit of volleyball instruction the learner will be able to:
1. Practice an adherence to the rules of the game of volleyball during competition.

2. Demonstrate an interest in self-improvement by using available time before and after class to practice the skills being learned.

3. Demonstrate a sensitivity to others by encouraging each member of a team to participate freely and without fear of failure.

4. Write a personal physical fitness program and explain how volleyball participation can be an important part of the program.

Personal-Social Domain Objectives

As a result of participation in a unit of volleyball instruction, the learner will be able to:

1. Listen attentively when the teacher is introducing a new skill or another student is asking a question.

2. Practice forearm passing the volleyball with a partner for a full five minutes.

3. Demonstrate in a game situation that he or she can play his or her own position and allow the other players to do the same.

4. Set the ball to both on-hand and off-hand positions, allowing more than one individual the opportunity to spike the ball.

5. Identify the first names of all members of his or her team and 50 percent of the names of all other members of the class.

SUGGESTED STUDENT PROJECTS

1. Construct a set of logical performance objectives for a beginning class in volleyball; consider all five objective areas; and use chapter 8 (Evaluation) for identifying levels of criteria for performance.

2. Look at one or more of the books listed in the References for this chapter. Do any of these books help you in identifying realistic performance objectives?

3. Interview a local junior high school or high school teacher of volleyball. What advice does he or she give on identifying realistic performance objectives?

REFERENCES

Bloom, B.S.; M.D. Englehart; E.J. Furst; W.J. Hill; and D.R. Krathwohl. *Taxonomy of Educational Objectives, Handbook I: The Cognitive Domain.* New York: David McKay Co., 1956.

Corbin, C.B. *Becoming Physically Educated in the Elementary School.* Philadelphia: Lea and Febiger, 1976.

Corbin, C.V. *A Textbook of Motor Development.* Dubuque, Iowa: Wm. C. Brown Co. Publishers, 1980.

Krathwohl, D.R.; B.S. Bloom; and B.B. Masia. *Taxonomy of Educational Objectives, Handbook II: Affective Domain.* New York: David McKay Co., 1964.

Mager, R.F. *Preparing Instructional Objectives.* Palo Alto, California: Fearson Publishers, Inc., 1962.

Neilson, N.P., and A.O. Bronson. *Problems in Physical Education.* Englewood Cliffs, New Jersey: Prentice-Hall, Inc., 1965.

3

Organization

The purpose of this chapter is to provide the teacher with ideas for effectively implementing the instructional program. Specifically, the following topics will be considered: (a) the daily lesson plan, (b) the first teaching period (roll call and equipment set-up), (c) student leadership, (d) group size for drills, (e) instructional units, and (f) large-group instruction.

THE DAILY LESSON PLAN

The introductory sections of chapters 5, 6, and 7 outline a series of teaching progressions for instructing beginning, intermediate, and advanced-level students, respectively. Each of these progressions provides the teacher with a general outline of topics to be covered during a specified period of instruction, and from this outline, the teacher is expected to construct a lesson plan for each specific unit of instruction. For example, if the progression calls for a micro-unit of instruction on forearm passing, the instructor would compose a daily lesson plan on that subject.

If properly composed and utilized, the daily lesson plan can be an invaluable tool in helping each student achieve performance objectives. While the nature of a daily lesson plan may vary from teacher to teacher, there are three basic guidelines that should be followed. First, keep the lesson plan simple and to the point; second, allow for flexibility in instruction; and third, make the utilization of the lesson plan a daily habit. A sample lesson plan for teaching a unit of instruction on the forearm pass is presented in Box 3.1.

THE FIRST TEACHING PERIOD

Procedures for roll call and the setting up and taking down of nets and standards are the two critical topics that must be clarified during the first teaching period. Other items of lesser importance that might be clarified are (a) acceptable wearing apparel, (b) attendance expectations, (c) starting and stopping times, (d) care of equipment, and (e) procedures for checking out locker and towel.

Roll Call

The monitoring of student attendance is an important part of the instructional process in schools (although of lesser importance in a YMCA or recreational setting). Roll call procedures, however,

BOX 3.1.
THE DAILY LESSON PLAN

TOPIC: *The forearm pass in volleyball.*

Content of Topic

1. Ready position.
2. Handclasp technique.
3. Lock elbows upon contact.
4. Contact point.
5. Use legs for power.

Performance Objectives–Students will be able to:

1. Keep elbows locked in executing the pass.
2. Earn a score of 20 on the Brumbach wall-volley test.
3. Utilize the pass in a game situation.

Learning Experiences (drills)

1. Toss and bump drill.
2. Passing back and forth.
3. Bump to self and then to partner.
4. Pass served balls in game situation.

Time Schedule

9:30 – 9:35	Lecture and demonstration
9:35 – 9:40	Drill 1
9:40 – 9:45	Drill 2
9:45 – 9:50	Drill 3
9:50 – 10:00	Drill 4
10:00 – 10:10	Administer Brumbach test

should be carried out quickly since time is of the essence. Several methods for speeding up the roll call process will be discussed briefly, and a method recommended for volleyball instruction will be outlined.

In most situations, the traditional method of *calling names* is the least desirable method of checking attendance. This is especially true when the student population is large (45 to 60 students per instructor). In the *verbal numbers* system, each student is assigned a personal number. At the proper time, each student responds verbally with his or her assigned number in consecutive order. If a pause occurs after a particular number, the instructor assumes an absence, calls that number out loud, and makes a pencil notation of the absence. While this system is more time efficient than the name-calling procedure, it tends to depersonalize people. In a third method, the *visual numbers* system, each student is assigned a numbered position on the floor or against a wall (benches in many basketball and football stadiums are marked numerically). In this case, when the instructor asks for roll call, the students move to a position against a wall in front of or standing on their assigned number. Absent students are easily noted because of open spaces and visible numbers.

With the *student cluster* roll call system, students are assigned to a particular student group. These groupings may vary anywhere from four students per group to as many as ten. Each group is assigned a leader who is responsible for reporting absences in his or her group. Each group is also assigned a place on the gym floor or field to line up behind their leader for roll call. In practice, the instructor calls roll by merely asking each leader to report the names of absent members. This is a good system, since not only does it save valuable time, but it assists the students (especially the group leader) in becoming acquainted with group members. The obvious sociological aspects of this system should be expanded by changing the leaders as well as the composition of the groups from time to time.

The roll call procedure recommended for volleyball instruction is called the *team-group method*. This method has many of the characteristics of the cluster-group concept, but has carry-over potential into class instruction and organization. In this system, it is not necessary to take time for roll call at all. Rather, students are assigned to various six-person teams with one member designated as team captain.

An important component of the team concept is to encourage students to join in actual team play as soon as they arrive in their class. This can be easily arranged by posting opponent and court assignment before class begins. In this way, students enter the gym, note their court assignment, and begin playing volleyball without any loss of playing time. When you (the instructor) are ready to take roll, you merely walk from court to court, noting teams with absences and asking team captains for assistance in identifying absent students. This can all be done in a few minutes with practically no interruption in team play.

There are other advantages of this system. For one, students are already organized into units for drill instruction with preassigned areas for practice. A second valuable advantage is the fact that team members get acquainted with each other. Also, as with the student cluster method, the sociological aspects of this system can be expanded by changing team groupings and team captains.

UTILIZATION OF STUDENT LEADERSHIP

There are numerous imaginative ways in which students can be utilized in leadership roles in a volleyball class. This utilization should be promoted for a couple of reasons. First, students can be of major value in improving the quality of instruction. Second, the students themselves can gain invaluable experience and confidence from making worthwhile contributions to the class. For this reason, all students, if possible, should be cast in a leadership role sometime during the volleyball unit.

Using students as group or team captains is beneficial to the teacher in terms of class organization and roll call procedures. The sharing of the opportunity to be a team captain should be encouraged and even legislated from time to time by you as the teacher. The changing of the group leader ought to take place when team memberships are realigned. The selection of the group leader can be made in several different ways. The instructor can appoint team captains who have volleyball experience or leadership ability, or the team captains can be chosen by the teams themselves.

Students should also be asked to put up the volleyball nets and standards. This experience gives each student some responsibility and also provides important knowledge about volleyball (care and use of equipment). In this particular aspect, if class members are assigned to teams and specific courts for instruction and play, students on a particular court should be responsible for the equipment on that court (i.e., putting up and taking down nets and standards properly).

A final way in which to involve students is in skill demonstrations. This can be done in one of two ways. First, highly skilled students can be called up to serve as "ideal" models of performance, a great morale booster for the selected students and a means of providing interest for the other members of the class. Secondly, students with beginning skill levels should be asked to assist in demonstrating how particular skills and learning experiences should be conducted. What is important is that each student be given a chance to contribute to the total success of the class.

SIZE OF GROUPS FOR DRILLS

From the standpoint of learning efficiency, the smaller the practice unit the better. Two people volleying a ball will be able to practice a particular skill a couple hundred times in less than ten minutes. In the same amount of time, a drill group involving six people and one ball will only receive approximately a third of the practice attempts afforded the smaller practice group. The major limitation for using small practice groups will be a scarcity of volleyballs. The instructor must ensure that enough balls are available for maximum learning. Several suggestions for obtaining a sufficient number of volleyballs for practice purposes have been outlined in chapter 4.

While small groups (two or three per ball) are best for practicing specific skill fundamentals, larger groups are often ideal for lead-up game skills. For example, a lead-up game drill for practicing service reception as a team might involve as many as twelve players (see drill section of chapter 5). The team-groups (six persons per team) described under roll call procedures can be used to form drill groups of two, three, four, six, and twelve players, involving team-group members on both sides of the net.

MICRO-UNIT OF INSTRUCTION

The micro-unit of instruction approach to teaching volleyball will be recommended in this text. This approach (used equally well for beginning, intermediate, or advanced levels) encourages a maximum amount of volleyball participation without sacrificing important units of instruction.

The micro-unit of instruction approach differs from a recreational approach in that students receive instruction on needed phases of the game as opposed to merely playing the game. Many of the positive aspects of the recreational approach, however, are retained (relaxed environment, opportunities for play, and freedom from pressures for a grade). In the recreational approach to teaching volleyball, the instructor does not distinguish between the development of specific skills and the game situation itself (learning drills and lead-up games). Rather, the instructor may call the class together for a brief verbal and physical demonstration of a particular skill. Afterwards, the students are sent back to their respective courts with the recommendation to try out the new techniques. However, without some organized opportunity to practice the new skill, it is unlikely that the student will gain acceptable proficiency (Wickstrom, 1967).

The micro-unit of instruction approach differs from a drill-oriented approach in that the use of drills for practice is secondary in importance to actual game participation. The drill-oriented approach is similar to part-learning strategy in that individual components of the game must be mastered (through drills) prior to actual game participation (Lawther, 1968). The basic problem with the drill-oriented instructional approach, however, is that it gets low marks in terms of motivating students. Students generally take a course in volleyball to learn and to have fun. The fun part is often lacking if the emphasis in the class is upon skill development through drill.

In the micro-unit of instruction, the advantages of both the recreational and the drill-oriented approaches are combined. The important components are summarized in the following list:

1. The students become involved in actual game participation as soon as they understand the objective of the game.

2. According to predetermined progression, students are introduced to new skills and concepts through micro-units of instruction.

3. A micro-unit of instruction incorporates such things as a verbal description, live demonstration, question and answer period, and drills for practice.

4. A micro-unit of instruction should not take up the entire class period, but should allow time at the beginning and end of the period for practice in the game situation.

5. Once a new skill or concept has been introduced to a class, the instructor must insist upon its utilization in the actual game. For example, once the forearm pass for reception has been demonstrated, all improper methods of playing the ball below the waist (lifting the ball with open fingers and hands) are discouraged. Team captains and/or referees (if used) will monitor this process.

6. If acceptable (in the instructor's judgment) learning does not materialize after a micro-unit of instruction, additional instructional sessions can be introduced to encourage skill development.

7. Films, video tapes, special demonstrations, and field trips (e.g., a local USVBA club team practice) can all be incorporated into individual micro-units of instruction.

In the micro-unit of instruction approach, students are continually participating in the total game situation, but from time to time they are drawn together for specific instruction, demonstration, and practice on important phases of the game. Mastery of one skill of the game must not be insisted upon before students move on to another. However, if acceptable progress is not being made on any particular part of the game, a second, third, and even fourth micro-unit of instruction can be given on that particular skill or concept. All necessary skills and concepts should be completely introduced as early as possible. In general, the goal of the teacher is to get the students playing the game in its proper form as rapidly as possible.

ORGANIZATION FOR LARGE-GROUP INSTRUCTION

Organization of class members into team groups for play, roll call, and practice drills has already been discussed in this chapter. Details for the organization of students for specific drills will be discussed in the appropriate sections of chapters 5, 6, and 7. Although nothing has been said, yet, about organizing an entire class (30-45 students) for purposes of discussion, illustration, and demonstration, the essential key is common sense. Sometimes, in actual practice, the beginning teacher can get so wrapped up in the content of his or her unit of instruction that consideration of such a basic item as group organization is passed over.

The following list indicates some of the basic considerations necessary for properly organizing a large group of students for instruction:

1. The overall concern of the teacher should be that every student be situated so as to see and hear clearly everything that goes on.

2. Before commencing the presentation, the instructor should insist that *all* students be sitting and paying attention.

3. If instruction is taking place out-of-doors, students should be arranged so that neither they nor the instructor look directly into the sun. In some cases, this can be a problem in an indoor facility as well.

4. For volleyball instruction, an ideal group configuration is a U-shaped configuration with the instructor at the open end of the U. The best way to arrange this is to have students sit down outside the back two-thirds of a volleyball court (see Figure 3.1).

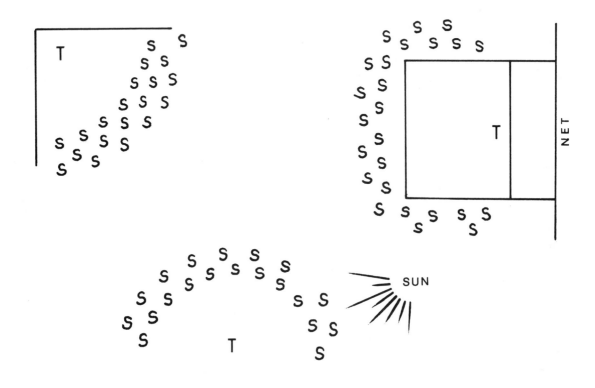

FIGURE 3.1

5. When organizing large groups of students into drills, do so systematically.

6. If the acoustics of a building are particularly poor, or if a facility is being shared with another class, it is often advisable to have the students sit in a semicircle facing one corner of the facility (the instructor then stands in the corner).

7. While the U and semicircle configurations are generally the most effective for large group demonstrations and discussion, the complete circle (instructor surrounded) is probably the worst, because the instructor will always have his or her back to many of the students.

8. Regardless of how the class is organized for large group instruction, always consider the problem prior to entering the classroom. Last-minute decisions are often poor decisions.

SUGGESTED STUDENT PROJECTS

1. Develop a daily lesson plan for the first day of instruction for an intermediate volleyball class.

2. List ten ways in which you as an instructor can utilize student leadership in the teaching process.

3. Figure 3.1 suggests ways of organizing large groups of students for instruction. Can you diagram other configurations that might be used?

REFERENCES

Lawther, J.D. *The Learning of Physical Skills.* Englewood Cliffs, New Jersey: Prentice-Hall, Inc., 1968.

Wickstrom, R.L. "In Defense of Drills." *The Physical Educator,* 24 (1967), 39-40.

Equipping the Volleyball Facility

Occasionally, the volleyball teacher will have an opportunity to assist administrators and building planners in designing the physical layout for volleyball instruction. Such considerations as court spacing, ceiling height, selection, and placement of nets and standards are of prime importance. Informed input from a knowledgeable teacher can make the difference between having a poor or an excellent teaching facility.

While the teacher does not always have the opportunity to be involved in the basic plan of the teaching facility, he or she often has a great deal to say about the selection, maintenance, set-up, and storage of such basic equipment as volleyballs, volleyball standards, and nets. Chapter 4 will discuss the different ways for planning and setting up a volleyball teaching facility.

THE VOLLEYBALL FACILITY

Rarely is a physical education facility designed with volleyball in mind. Usually, a facility is designed for basketball and only secondarily for such sports as volleyball, badminton, team handball, or indoor tennis. In actuality, a basketball facility can also be made into an excellent volleyball facility if the following alterations and considerations can be implemented. (See Figure 4.1).

1. Install basketball goals that can be elevated or retracted off the playing area.

2. Design a ceiling that allows 9.1 meters (about 30 ft) of clearance from floor to any ceiling obstruction.

3. When designing partitions (netting or solid) to separate a large gym area into smaller teaching stations, consider volleyball as well as basketball in terms of court placement.

4. Surround the gymnasium area with smooth, unobstructed wall surfaces to a height of at least 6.1 meters (about 20 ft). These smooth, durable, and unobstructed surfaces can be used for volley practice stations.

5. Arrange the volleyball courts so that a minimum of six feet is allowed between adjacent playing courts, and between out-of-bounds lines and walls.

6. Lay out a single championship court in the center of a spectator seating area for use in intramural, interscholastic, or USVBA championship matches.

7. Install a hardwood or smooth synthetic floor. Since volleyball players typically do a lot of floor work in diving and rolling for balls, an abrasive or rough floor surface should be avoided.

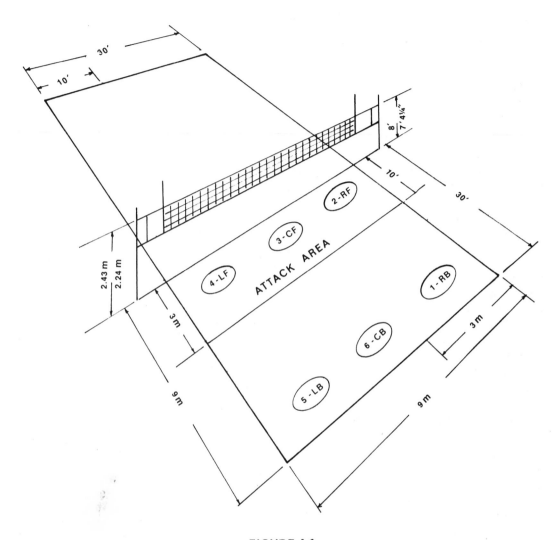

FIGURE 4.1

8. Countersink floor plates in the concrete underlying a hardwood floor surface. Failure to do this will result in damage to the playing surface whenever tension is placed on the cable running from floor to volleyball standard.

NET STANDARDS

In order to set up nets for proper volleyball instruction, it is necessary to have a set of durable standards. These volleyball standards must be secured in some manner to ensure constant tension on the suspended volleyball net. Such half measures as using poles that are inserted into cement-filled rubber tires are *not* acceptable for volleyball instruction. On the other hand, sophisticated and expensive rigging that is sometimes purchased is generally unnecessary.

The following basic guidelines may be considered in selecting volleyball net standards:

1. The net standards and system for securing the standard to the floor (or wall) should be simple. Extra floor cables, complex myriads of pulleys, handles, and levers are all unnecessary.

2. The volleyball rigging system should allow for speedy set-up and take-down. Net systems that require several workers and more than five minutes of time to set up must be considered inefficient.

3. The expense of purchasing standards can be somewhat curtailed by buying component parts (cables, take-up reels, and accessories) and assembling them later. In fact, if a metal workshop is available (school workshop), much of the fitting work could be done there.

4. While floor bases that require screw-in floor plates are most common, the use and purchase of balanced bases is very practical. The standards are easily moved for storage and can be used for badminton and tennis. If balanced bases are used, heavy-duty casters should be attached for easy moving and placement.

5. While most net-standard systems require floor cables, cable insertion plates, and screw-in floor plates for the standard base, some of the newer systems utilize only heavy-duty construction and a floor sleeve. These systems are generally quite expensive, but also very safe.

NET SELECTION

Proper net selection is as important as the selection of volleyball standards. While nets should be simple in construction, easy to set up, and relatively inexpensive, the volleyball teacher must insist upon the purchase and selection of nets that can be set up according to rule book specifications. Generally speaking, four kinds of nets can be purchased: (1) cloth nets, with rope at top and bottom for tension control; (2) lightweight netting, with small steel cable (about $\frac{1}{8}$ in.) on top and lightweight rope on the bottom; (3) heavy-duty netting, with heavy steel cable (about $\frac{1}{4}$ to $\frac{1}{3}$ in.) on top and heavy nylon rope on the bottom; and (4) heavy-duty netting, with heavy steel cable top and bottom. Information regarding the selection of each of these net types is given in Table 4.1.

HINTS FOR EASY SET-UP AND TAKE-DOWN

Regardless of what sort of volleyball standard and net system is employed (assuming it is simple), there are a number of worthwhile teaching tips that can make the process of set-up and take-down easier. See Figure 4.2.

Single-Cable System

Unless a heavy-duty, cableless, sleeve system is used, the single-cable system for providing tension and stability to the standard is desirable. First of all, it is safer for the students. A two-cable system is complicated and invites injury due to tripping. Second, a single cable allows for much quicker set-up than does the two-cable system.

A sample system using a single steel-cable guideline is illustrated in Figure 4.2. In this illustration, it can be observed that a number of component parts make up the floor-to-standard cable. Each of these component parts (latch hook, turnbuckle, section of chain, and key hooks) allows for quick and easy cable length adjustment. Since the component parts of this cable linkage system can be easily misplaced, it is important to store the entire cable guideline in a secure place near the court.

TABLE 4.1
NET SELECTION

NET TYPE	COMMENTS
1. Cloth net, rope on top and bottom.	Not suitable for quality indoor instruction. Difficult to provide proper height and tension. Recommended for outdoor recreation.
2. Lightweight, small steel cable on top and rope on bottom.	Suitable for volleyball instruction. Relatively inexpensive and easy to set up. Heavy-duty nylon straps instead of steel cable may be used as guidelines from floor to standard. Durability of net is a limitation.
3. Heavy-duty, large steel cable on top and rope on bottom.	Requires only one take-up reel. Very durable and acceptable for both instruction and competition purposes.
4. Heavy-duty, large steel cable on top and bottom.	Requires two take-up reels. Extremely durable, but difficult to manage (not versatile).

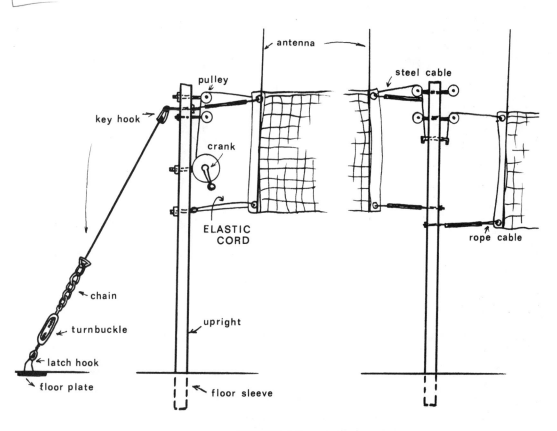

FIGURE 4.2

As mentioned previously, if a lightweight net with $\frac{1}{8}$-inch steel tension cable is used, it is possible to use heavy-duty nylon adjustable marine straps (see the list of vendors on pp. 19-20). While the use of these 2-inch-wide straps is uncommon, they have proven to be strong, durable, and extremely convenient.

Providing Net Tension

As shown in Figure 4.2, a hand crank take-up reel is used to provide tension on top of the net cable. This crank reel should be durable and of high-quality construction to withstand constant stress and tension. The crank reel must be firmly attached to the pole upright with heavy-duty bolts. The end of the net cable should be looped for easy connection to pole standard and reel (frayed ends can be neatly and safely taped).

As indicated in Figure 4.2, the steel net cable passes through one of two pulleys to get to the take-up reel. These two heavy-duty pulleys must be secured to the volleyball standard to allow a net height of 2.43 meters (about 8 ft) for men and 2.24 meters (about 7 ft 4¼ in.) for women. Since the placement of these pulleys will determine the height of the net, they should be attached to the standard at a height of approximately 2.48 meters for men and 2.29 meters for women. This is because the rotation of the pulley at its attachment will lower the height of the net. If the pulleys are stationary, or the cable passes through a fixed U-shaped attachment, it is not necessary to allow for the deflection of the pulley. However, failure to use a pulley will accelerate the wear and tear on the net cable.

Net tension on the bottom of the net is accomplished by tying the rope cable to the appropriate attachment on the upright. At least two lower net cable attachments should be bolted into place, one spaced to accommodate a men's net and the other a women's.

When both top and bottom net cables have been secured, the net itself will be free to slide laterally on the cables (like a towel draped over a taut clothes line). The net itself is secured in position by using nylon cord ($\frac{1}{8}$ in. in diameter), or heavy elastic rope with hook attachments on the ends. These elastic cords (similar to those used on a trampoline) are very convenient for use in volleyball net adjustment. While they do not provide the stability required for competition, they are more than adequate for instructional purposes.

While a take-up reel is necessary for providing tension on a steel cable, it is not necessary to have two of them. Figure 2.1 shows that the right aspect of the net merely attaches to a hook that protrudes from the upright. This upright could serve as the center pole between two courts.

The out-of-bounds antennas shown in the illustration are not necessary for classroom instruction. They are, however, required for competition. In HFSHSA rules, the antennas are placed 8½ inches outside the vertical tape markers. In USVBA and NAGWS rules, the antennas are placed on the outside aspect of the tape markers (out-of-bounds line).

Set-up and Storage

For setting up the volleyball nets and standards, the following steps are recommended:

1. Place all standards in proper positions. Make sure that standards that have take-up reels are placed on the outside position of a series of courts and those without the reel are placed between courts. If pole standards are used that fit into a floor sleeve, or are attached (hand bolt) to the floor in some manner, the placement of standards is predetermined.

2. Attach steel cables running from floor to standard. Make necessary adjustments on chain linkage and turnbuckle. Again, if placement of the standard is predetermined by a floor attachment, the floor-to-standard cable will be standard length (no chain linkage or turnbuckle). When in position, the cable should be taut and the upright inclined slightly away from the court.

3. Attach top steel cable of net to the two uprights. Turn hand crank until the net is strung tight.

4. Check to make sure that net is at proper height and that uprights are perpendicular to the floor. Make minor adjustments on take-up reel and turnbuckles to assure this.

5. Secure bottom of net rope cables to standards (make sure the rope is taut). If steel cable is used, secure to and tighten with a take-up reel.

6. Slide net into position laterally by lining up vertical tape markers with out-of-bounds line. Attach net to standards by using prepared elastic cords.

7. Attach net antennas (if being used).

8. In taking the nets down, start by removing net antennas and work backwards on this list. Note that these steps are generally applicable regardless of the type of rigging used (eliminate step 2 if a cableless system is used).

When volleyball standards are not being used, they should be either removed from the gym floor or stored safely. Improperly stored equipment could be a cause for a law suit, as tripping or falling on the standards can cause injury.

Volleyball nets are best stored by hanging them on hooks attached to the wall. Several nets can be draped on the same hooks. When volleyball instruction (and play) is over for the season, the nets should be folded away for storage.

COMPETITION VOLLEYBALL RIGGING

Some organizations will be interested in purchasing high-quality volleyball equipment for competition and/or instructional purposes. Although the initial cost may be substantial, it is less important than the factors of durability and simplicity.

If your school or organization is in the process of purchasing high-quality volleyball equipment, consider the list of vendors in this chapter. Write the manufacturers and request an equipment catalogue. There are many fine volleyball rigging systems on the market today. The most promising systems being marketed are those that do not require the use of any sort of floor-to-standard (upright) guidelines. These systems employ heavy-duty, height-adjustable uprights that fit into a sleeve built into the floor. This type of rigging, extremely versatile and durable, is currently manufactured by Senoh Corporation of Japan. The Aero Instrument Company also sells a system that does not require floor-to-standard cables. However, their product uses lightweight $\frac{1}{8}$-inch cable nets and would not be adequate for a ¼-inch steel-cable competition net.

The following is a list of vendors of volleyball equipment:

Aero Instrument Company, Inc.
6935 Stearns
Houston, Texas 77021

Excel Sports Products, Inc.
P.O. Box 3153
Auburn, California 95604
(Various volleyball teaching aids, nets, and net accessories, but no standards)

GSC Athletic Equipment
600 North Pacific Avenue
San Pedro, California 90733

Jayfro Corporation
P.O. Box 400
Waterford, Connecticut 06385

H.E. Wilson & Co. Volleyballs
Box 77065
San Francisco, California 94107
(Volleyball nets and accessories,
but no standards)

Nissen Gymnasium Company
930 — 27th Avenue SW
Cedar Rapids, Iowa 52406

Paul J. Barnes
Volleyball Equipment
1859 South Madison Street
Denver, Colorado 80210

PCA Industries, Inc.
2298 Grisson Drive
St. Louis, Missouri 63141

Rawlings Sporting Goods Co.
2300 Delmar Blvd.
St. Louis, Missouri 63166

Senoh Sports Imports, Inc.
P.O. Box 5608
Columbus, Ohio 43221

Sports Merchant
Box 240
North Boston, New York 14110

Sports Pal Company, Inc.
P.O. Box 28906
St. Louis, Missouri 63132

United Marine Company
4800 Blue Parkway
Kansas City, Missouri 64130
(Carry the heavy-duty 2-inch-wide nylon straps)

Victory Sports Nets
Division of FNT Industries, Inc.
927 First Street
Menominee, Michigan 49858
(Nets and accessories only, no standards)

West Coast Netting, Inc.
14929 Clark Avenue
City of Industry, California 91745

CARE AND SELECTION OF VOLLEYBALLS

A prime consideration in volleyball instruction is the volleyball. The experienced teacher can provide a great deal of instruction with only a volleyball. For example, the skills of forearm passing, setting, face passing, diving, and rolling can all be practiced and learned in the absence of nets and standards.

Selection

From an instructional point of view, almost any kind of leather volleyball is acceptable. However, from a competition standpoint, this is not true. Both USVBA (1979) and the NFSHSA (1978-79) publish a list of "approved volleyballs." Listed in Table 4.2 are volleyballs that are on the approved list for both organizations. The NFSHSA further differentiates by stating that the Molten ball (V-58L and V-58SL) is the official volleyball of this organization.

TABLE 4.2
APPROVED LIST OF VOLLEYBALLS

USVBA	NFSHSA
Brine LVB (18)*	Adidas "Volley-I" (18)
Brine SVB (18)	Game Master GMI-17 (12)
Dura Play VBL 381 (18)	Game Master GMI-16 (18)
Mikasa VL200 (18)	Game Master GMI-16P (18)
Molten RMV5-18 (18)	Jaguar VB-25 (18)
Peerless VB50 (18)	Jaguar VB-50 (18)
Regent 79000 (18)	Mikasa NF200 (18)
Spalding Elite	Molten V-58L (18)
Tachikara SV-5W Gold (18)	Sportcraft 23288 (18)
Tachikara SV-5WS (18)	Sportcraft 23280 (12)
Tachikara SV-5 Star (12)	Tachikara SV-5W (18)
VOIT CV404	Tachikara KV-18 (18)
VOIT XV404	Zasco 18-K (18)

*Number of panels noted in parentheses.

Generally speaking, the following features should be considered in selecting volleyballs for classroom instruction:

1. Volleyballs should have a leather cover. Rubber and plastic-covered balls are not recommended for indoor instructional purposes. While rubber balls last a long time, they have a different bounce from leather balls, and they tend to "sting" the arm when forearm passing is practiced. Beginners do not like to practice forearm passing with rubber volleyballs!

2. Volleyballs should be of a molded construction. The old-style leather volleyballs with stitched paneling are outdated because they had a tendency to lose their shape and to expand with use. The molded construction has generally alleviated this problem.

3. A volleyball that has a bladder separate from the leather and cloth-lined casing should be selected. Balls that employ this feature have a "softer touch," which is important to volleyball players.

4. The cost should be considered in selecting volleyballs. It is best to compose a list of balls that are acceptable, ask for bids on bulk amounts, and be prepared to analyze returned bids.

Other Considerations

Ball care. Volleyballs should be stored in a cloth bag (fish netting) that allows for circulation of air among the balls. The ball bags should be hung off the floor in a well-ventilated storage area. Students should be reminded not to sit on or kick the volleyballs. The prime culprit in prematurely aging a volleyball is moisture. If balls become damp from water or sweat, they should be immediately dried off with a dry towel. Leather conditioner, if used sparingly, can help keep the balls in good shape.

Ball acquisition. A well-equipped volleyball class will have at least one ball for every four students. If possible, enough balls should be available for every pair of students.

Sometimes the failure to have enough balls available for quality instruction is due to a scarcity of funds. If this is the case, the following suggestions might help the instructor procure more volleyballs:

1. Take your problem directly to the principal and/or superintendent. Explain to him or her that more balls will encourage greater participation among students and that greater participation will enhance skill learning as well as the physical fitness of the students.

2. Approach coaches of volleyball athletic teams in your area. College and sometimes high school athletic teams discard their worn-out volleyballs at the end of a season. Many of the volleyballs that they consider worn out may be more than acceptable to your class.

3. Explain the problem to the students since some of them may be able to bring balls from home.

4. Explain your problem to local sporting goods stores. Give them the opportunity to bid on a dozen or so balls. Often, they will donate a few balls as a service to the community.

Inventory. Once you have enough volleyballs for instructional purposes, keep them. The best ways to accomplish this are to identify and number all balls with a black felt-tip pen; to keep a written inventory of all your equipment, including the number of volleyballs; to check volleyballs out to squad leaders or student assistants; and finally, to insist that all balls be accounted for before class is dismissed.

List of Vendors

The following vendors carry the volleyballs that are listed as USVA-approved volleyballs in Table 4.2:

AMF VOIT, Inc.
3801 S. Harbor Blvd.
Santa Ana, California 92702

Arch Billmire, Inc.
2650 Third Street
San Francisco, California 94107
(Tachikara)

General Sportcraft Co., Ltd.
140 Woodline Street
Bergenfield, New Jersey 07621

Jaguar Products, Inc.
P.O Box 455
Brentwood, New York 11717
(Peerless)

Molten Industrial Rubber Co.
Mr. Wayne Mills, Authorized Representative
R&M Athletic Equipment Company
P.O. Box 65
Valley Center, California 92082

Regent Sports Corporation
45 Ranick Road
Hauppauge, New York 11787

Spalding, Division of Questor
Meadow Street
Chicopee, Massachusetts 01014

Sport Fun, Inc.
4621 Sperry Street
Los Angeles, California 90039
(Dura Play)

Sports and Leisure International
711 West 17th Street, #D11
Costa Mesa, California 92627
(Mikasa)

W.H. Brine Company
1450 Highland Ave.
Needham, Massachusetts 02192

SUGGESTED STUDENT PROJECTS

1. Diagram your high school gym. Indicate an ideal "set-up" for volleyball in that facility.

2. Send for at least one catalogue that gives information about volleyball equipment.

3. Investigate at least three different catalogues. Get description and price estimates of volleyball standards, nets, and volleyballs you consider best.

4. Thinking again of your own high school facility, describe how you might adequately store nets, balls, and standards.

REFERENCES

NFHSA. *Volleyball Rule Book (1978-79).* Elgin, Illinois: National Federation of State High School Associations, 1978.

USVBA. *1979 Official Volleyball Rules.* San Francisco: United States Volleyball Association, 1978.

Volleyball Instruction for Beginners

This chapter (as well as chapters 6 and 7) on teaching volleyball to beginners will be composed of three main sections. Section one: a sample teaching progression designed for 30 or 20 micro-units of instruction. The micro-units making up the progressions may be considered somewhat synonymous with days. A number of the skill and team strategy elements outlined in the progression will be covered in greater detail in sections two and three. Section two: elaboration on techniques of teaching the fundamental skills outlined in the progressions. This section will be further broken down into skill execution and drills for practice. Section three: discussion of the execution and teaching of several of the team strategies of play that have been outlined in the progression.

SAMPLE TEACHING PROGRESSION

This progression is composed of 30 micro-units of instruction. By eliminating the micro-units that are marked with an asterisk (*), the progression may be shortened to 20 micro-units (days). The full 30-day progression is rather complete and allows sufficient time for skill development; skill, knowledge, and fitness testing; and intra-class competition.

Micro-Unit 1. Class organization
  a. Introductions.
  b. Attendance and grading procedures.
  c. Required wearing apparel, shower and locker room procedures.
  d. Instruction on set-up and take-down of nets.
  e. Organization into team groups.
  f. Explain roll call procedures.

Micro-Unit 2. Introduction to volleyball
  a. Show brief film on volleyball or provide live demonstration.
  b. Distribute a copy of basic rules of play. Permission of author is granted to make copies of the rules listed in Box 5.1.
  c. Students play volleyball. Instructor observes general knowledge and level of play exhibited.

BOX 5.1
BASIC VOLLEYBALL RULES

1. The height of the net for girls and women is 2.24 meters (about 7 ft 4¼ in.) and for men and boys is 2.43 meters (about 8 ft).

2. A game is played to 15 points. The winning team must have a 2-point advantage. A match is the best 2 of 3 games.

3. The ball may be played by any part of the body above (and including) the waist.

4. While serving, the server may not step on the service line (foot fault).

5. Points are scored by the serving team only.

6. An illegal play is called when the ball is held (noticeably comes to rest).

7. An illegal play is called when the ball is hit twice in succession by the same player (see rules 8 and 9 for exceptions).

8. A player touching the ball while blocking may make the next play on the ball if it remains on his/her side of the net.

9. If a player contacts the ball twice in rapid succession while in the act of blocking, this counts as only one hit.

10. Multiple contacts by the block count as one hit.

11. A team is allowed three contacts of the ball (for exception, see rule 12).

12. A touch by the blocker(s) does not count as one of the team's three allowable hits.

13. Blocking with hands over the net is permissable as long as opponents are not interfered with in making their three attempts.

14. The net may not be touched while the ball (for exception, see rule 12).

15. The centerline (4 in. wide) may be touched but not the opponent's court (NFSHSA rules). In USVBA rules, the 2-inch wide centerline may be touched and opponent's court stepped on as long as some part of the player's foot is on or over the centerline.

16. A ball simultaneously held by two members of opposing teams is a play-over.

17. All players must be in their relative rotational positions at the instant the ball is served.

18. An overlap occurs (at time of serve) if a back-line player overlaps the immediate front-line player, or a player overlaps a player to his/her side.

19. Once the ball is in play, players may move to any position on the court.

20. Back-line players may not play a ball across the net if the ball is above the net, and the player is on or in front of the 3-meter (about 10-ft) spiking line (back-line spiker). It is legal if the player jumps from behind the spiking line and lands on or in front of it.

21. Back-line players may not participate in the act of blocking the ball back across the net.

Micro-Unit 3. The underhand floating serve
   a. Discussion.
   b. Demonstration.
   c. Drills for practice.
   d. Utilize underhand floating serve in game situation.

Micro-Unit 4. The forearm pass for service reception
   a. Discussion.
   b. Demonstration.
   c. Drills for practice.
   d. Utilize forearm pass for service reception in game situation.

*Micro-Unit 5. The forearm pass for service reception, continued
   a. Discussion.
   b. Drills for practice.
   c. Utilize forearm pass for service reception in game situation.

Micro-Unit 6. The W-receiving formation
   a. Discussion.
   b. Demonstration.
   c. Drills for practice.
   d. Utilize the W-receiving formation in game situation.

Micro-Unit 7. The face pass for setting
   a. Discussion.
   b. Demonstration.
   c. Drills for practice.
   d. Utilize face pass for setting forward in game situation.

*Micro-Unit 8. The face pass for setting, continued
   a. Discussion.
   b. Drills for practice.
   c. Utilize face pass for setting forward in game situation.

Micro-Unit 9. The basic power spike
   a. Discussion.
   b. Demonstartion.
   c. Drills for practice.
   d. Utilize spike in game situation.

*Micro-Unit 10. Review the basic power spike
   a. Discussion.
   b. Drills for practice.
   c. Utilize spike in game situation.

Micro-Unit 11. Introduce three-hit volleyball
   a. Lead-up game.
   b. Play game according to rules; each team, however, is penalized a point or side-out for failure to use all three allowable hits.

*Micro-Unit 12. Three-hit volleyball, continued

Micro-Unit 13. Play regular volleyball
  a. Encourage the use of three hits.
  b. Take notes on obvious areas of skill weaknesses.
  c. Instructor serves as a referee for approximately 10 minutes on each court.
    (1) Blow whistle only on obvious ball-handling errors.
    (2) Spend an equal amount of time on each court.
    (3) Encourage the use of proper skill techniques.

Micro-Unit 14. Testing and review
  a. Administer short true-false test on rules.
  b. Review skills taught.
  c. Provide mini-units of instruction on areas of skill deficiency.

Micro-Unit 15. Individual blocking technique
  a. Discussion.
  b. Demonstration.
  c. Drills for practice.
  d. Utilize the block in game situation.

Micro-Unit 16. Tandem blocking technique
  a. Discussion.
  b. Demonstration.
  c. Drills for practice.
  d. Utilize tandem blocking in game situation.

Micro-Unit 17. The 3-deep defense
  a. Discussion.
  b. Demonstration.
  c. Drills for practice.
  d. Utilize in game situation.

*Micro-Unit 18. Review 3-deep defense
  a. Discussion.
  b. Drills for practice.
  c. Utilize in game situation.

Micro-Unit 19. Defense-to-offense free-ball transition
  a. Discussion.
  b. Demonstration.
  c. Drills for practice.
  d. Practice in game situation.

*Micro-Unit 20. Play regular volleyball
  a. Instructor serves as a referee for 10 minutes on each court.
  b. Instructor looks for weaknesses in skill and team strategy.

*Micro-Unit 21. Review and provide mini-units of instruction on weak areas identified in Micro-Unit 20

*Micro-Unit 22. Intra-class volleyball tournament

*Micro-Unit 23. Intra-class volleyball tournament

*Micro-Unit 24. Intra-class volleyball tournament

Micro-Unit 25. Intra-class volleyball tournament

Micro-Unit 26. Intra-class volleyball tournament

Micro-Unit 27. Intra-class volleyball tournament

Micro-Unit 28. Volleyball skill testing (See chapter 8, Evaluation.)

Micro-Unit 29. Physical fitness testing (See chapter 8, Evaluation.)

Micro-Unit 30. Written examination on skill and team strategy techniques discussed during unit of instruction.

TEACHING THE FUNDAMENTAL SKILLS

Each of the fundamental skills covered in this section will be discussed in terms of execution and drills for practice. With regard to drill selection, it should be mentioned that a teacher does not have to use all drills listed for each skill, nor use all drills on the same day.

The Underhand Floating Serve

With beginners, it is important that they be successful at getting the ball into the opponents' court on the serve. Failure to do this results in a stalemate in learning since neither team gets an opportunity to practice the other phases of the game. For this reason, it is important that a relatively simple serve, such as the underhand floating serve, be taught early in the course. The floating serve is difficult to receive since it tends to follow an unpredictable course due to wind resistance on the surface of the ball. The deviations in the flight of the ball are usually one or two feet and therefore do not normally alter the basic accuracy of the serve.

Execution. The server starts by standing behind the service line in stride position. The leg opposite the hitting arm should be forward. The ball is held about waist level out in front of the lead leg. The hitting arm is extended at the elbow and is drawn backwards in preparation for the serve. In executing the hitting motion, the arm follows a path similar to one followed in pitching a horseshoe. At the same time the hitting arm is moving through its path, the body weight is being shifted forward from the trail to lead leg. The ball is contacted in front of the body at a point slightly below the waist. Immediately prior to hand contact with the ball, the ball is released by the nonhitting hand. Actual contact with the ball should take place on the heel of the open hand. Contact should be made squarely in the center of the ball. This will result in the ball traveling without any spin. The sequence of events involved in the underhand floating serve is illustrated in Photo Sequence 5.1.

Some members of the class will want to use an overhead floater serve. Since the development of an overhead serve is the ultimate objective in volleyball, this should be encouraged. If an overhead serve is used by some students, two criteria must be met: it must be accurate, and it must be playable by the receiving team. If the serve cannot be returned, the opponents will be unable to gain skill in returning the serve. This situation is as disruptive to the skill-learning objectives of the beginning course as failure to get the serve into the opponents' court.

Drills for practice. The following drills (in sequence) are suggested for use in developing skill in executing the underhand floating serve.

PHOTO SEQUENCE 5.1
The ready, release, contact, and follow-through phases of the underhand serve.

1. Wall serving drill. Learner stands about 9 meters (about 30 ft) from a flat-surfaced wall and practices serving the ball above 2.43-meter (about 8-ft) line marked on the wall. Students may be spaced 3 meters (about 10 ft) apart. One ball for every two or three people is needed.

2. Serving with partner (no net). (See Figure 5.1.) Students pair off facing each other across a volleyball court (sideline to sideline) and practice serving the ball back and forth. At its highest point, the flight of the ball should be about 4 meters (about 13 ft) above the floor. One ball for every two or four people is needed.

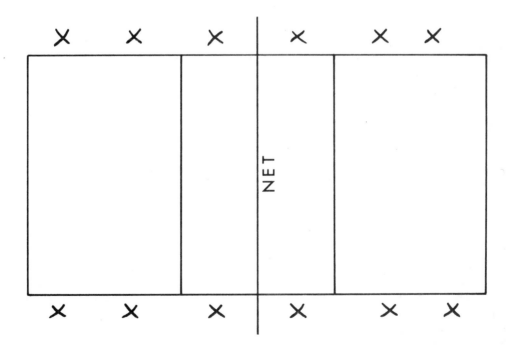

FIGURE 5.1

3. Serving with partner (across net). (See Figure 5.2.) Students pair off facing each other across a volleyball net while behind the baseline, and practice serving the ball back and forth across the net. Students are encouraged to serve deep and to clear the net by about 1.5 meters (about 5 ft). No more than six students should be behind a baseline, and one ball for every two people is needed.

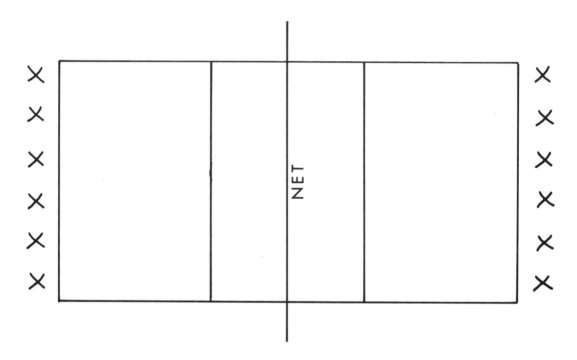

FIGURE 5.2

4. Service target test. (See Figure 5.3.) Students pair off facing each other behind their respective baselines and directly opposite one another. Players serve the ball back and forth until each has served 10 balls. The court is divided into three 3-meter (about 10-ft) strips extending from baseline to baseline. Each strip is further divided into three scoring zones. Students keep track of points and aim for target areas that result in the most points. Serves between partners must remain between 3-meter strips. Generally, the courts can be marked off using lines already on floor (tennis, basketball, and badminton lines).

The Forearm Pass for Service Reception

While the forearm pass is used in the game of volleyball for purposes of setting and digging, its primary function is service reception. When considered in this capacity, it is easily the most important skill in volleyball. This is simply because the first play of the ball (after the serve) sets the mood for all succeeding plays (e.g., an errant pass often results in an errant set).

Execution. In preparation for reception of an opponent's serve, the passer must be relaxed, in a stagger foot position, and with the weight of the body on the balls of the feet. When the ball is

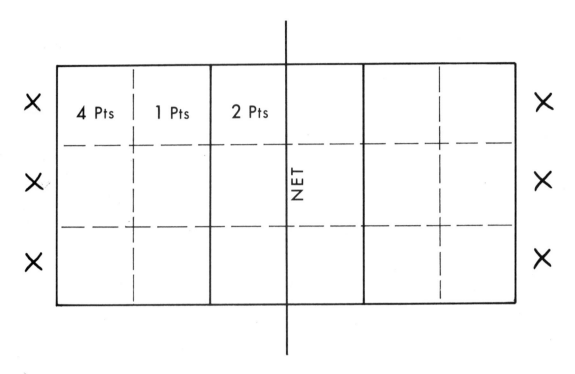

FIGURE 5.3

served, the receiver reacts to the ball by trying to get in a position directly in line with the ball. This is done by using small, quick, slide steps. In executing the slide steps, the knees are bent, but not so much that the passer's lateral quickness is impaired (if the passer's center of gravity is too low, he or she will be slow in lateral movement).

Actual contact with the ball by the passer takes place on the forearms, slightly above the wrist joint. Upon contact, the elbows are fully extended (arms straight) and the thumbs are pointed downward. The power for the forearm pass comes from culminating body forces (speed of ball, leg extension, hip extension, shoulder elevation, and shoulder flexion).

The forearm pass is best considered in terms of a "passing platform." With the elbows in a locked position and the thumbs and hands pointed downward, the arms are elevated, lowered, or tilted to provide the ball with a flat and appropriately inclined rebounding surface. The execution of the forearm pass is illustrated in Photo Sequence 5.2.

Drills for practice. The following drills (in sequence) are suggested for use in developing skill in executing the forearm pass.

1. Tossing and bumping drill. Students work in pairs with one person tossing and the other bumping the ball back to the tosser. The tosses should be made underhand and from a distance of no more than 3 meters (about 10 ft). Both the tosses and the bumps should be about 3 meters high. Partners should be spaced evenly over the available gym area.

2. Passing pairs. (See Figure 5.4.) Learners practice bumping the volleyball back and forth using the forearm pass. The ultimate goal should be to bump the ball 100 times without an error. Again,

PHOTO SEQUENCE 5.2
Forearm passing technique for service reception.

partners stand within 3 meters (about 10 ft) of each other and bump ball no higher than 3 meters above the floor. Drill may involve three people with one person in front passing to the other two.

3. Forearm pass to self and then to partner. Students bump a short, 1.5-meter (about 5-ft) pass to themselves and then a 3-meter-high pass to their partners. This is a ball-control drill and should be explained as such. The ultimate goal should be to bump the ball 50 times between partners.

4. Wall-volley forearm passing drill. Student stands in front of a flat wall and attempts to keep the ball in play above an 8-foot-high line drawn horizontal to the floor. To test them, ask students to see how many times they can volley against the wall in 60 seconds (Brumbach test).

5. Beginning service reception drill. (See Figure 5.5.) Learner takes a receiving position on the court and practices bumping balls to a setter standing by the net. Balls are thrown by a third person

FIGURE 5.4   FIGURE 5.5

from the middle of the opposite court. Each person receives ten tries and rotates. As many as four groups of three students may work on a net simultaneously.

6. Team service reception drill. (See Figure 5.6.) The player practices service reception in a team setting. The W-receiving formation is incorporated into the drill. This drill assists the players in identifying their areas of responsibility and in functioning as a team while passing as an individual. Each server (S) serves 25 balls (5 to each receiver). The receivers bump balls to the setter (#3 at this time), who sets the ball to the person standing in the on-hand hitting position (H). The hitter (H) tosses balls to a shagger (X) who gives balls to the feeder (F) who feeds the server. After 25 serves everyone rotates to a new position.

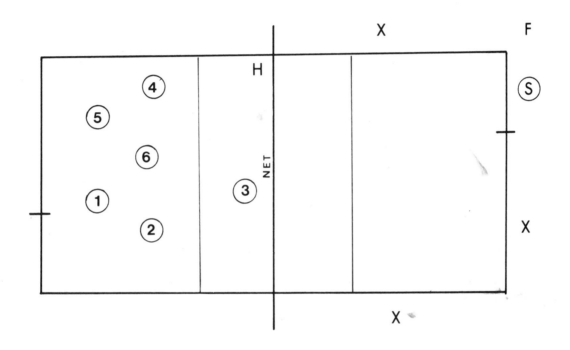

FIGURE 5.6

The Face Pass for Set

Prior to the 1964 Tokyo Olympics, the face pass was used almost exclusively for both setting and serve reception. Today, the face pass is used for setting, while the forearm pass is the primary method of receiving the serve. The change in service reception method came about primarily as change in the interpretation of the rules during the Olympics, as it was believed that a hard-driven serve could not be legally handled with a face pass. Consequently, the primary use of the face pass in modern volleyball is for setting the ball to the spiker.

Execution. In executing the face pass, the person moves in under the ball with knees bent and extends them as the ball is contacted with the fingers. Consequently, as in the forearm pass, a great deal of the power for the face pass comes from the legs. At the same time the person is moving under the ball, the hands are placed above the head with the elbows pointing down. The fingers are spread, the thumbs are nearly pointing at each other, and the wrists are extended or bent backwards. As the ball is contacted with the anterior or inside part of the fingertips, the wrists and fingers are flexed forward while the arms are extended at the elbow. Ball contact takes place only on the fingers and thumbs of the two hands. Improper handling of the ball includes not hitting the ball simultaneously with both hands (double hit), contacting the ball with the palms (catching), or directing the ball noticeably with the fingers. Correct execution of the face pass is illustrated in Photo Sequence 5.3.

PHOTO SEQUENCE 5.3
Face passing technique for setting the ball forward.

For proper setting of the ball, the feet should be in stride position (as opposed to square with each other), with the body moving in the direction of the set. The stride position allows the setter to step in the direction of the set. The most accurate sets can be made when the setter's body (front and back) is lined up in the direction of the set. With the emphasis in volleyball being upon handling the ball cleanly, it is easy for the beginner to get the idea that the face pass must be virtually "stabbed" with the fingers. However, a good face pass is really a *very fast* catch and throw. This is important for the beginner to understand, since it is literally impossible to stop the ball from coming to rest at some point. The rules state that it is an illegal set if the ball noticeably comes to rest on the setter's fingers. In today's modern game of volleyball, a great deal of latitude is allowed in setting the ball as long as the ball is cleanly handled and the setter has his or her body center of gravity underneath the ball. Of course, this is all a matter of judgment and is the reason for a referee. However, it is important that the beginner be given the latitude to learn the face pass without being called for lifting or double hitting all the time. As pointed out by Peppler (1977), volleyball is one game where the participant is penalized twice, once for poor technique (inaccurate set) and once for legality (loss of point).

Drills for practice. The following drills (in sequence) are suggested for use in developing skill in executing the face pass for set.

1-4. Drills 1 through 4 for setting are exactly like drills 1 through 4 for forearm passing (this chapter), except that the face pass is used instead of the bump. Consequently, they will not be repeated here.

5. Setting drill while sitting. (See Figure 5.7.) Partners face each other from sitting position. Legs are spread, feet of opposing partners are one meter (about 3 ft) apart. Learners practice setting the ball back and forth from this position. One ball is needed for each pair of students.

6. Setting and bumping drill. (See Figure 5.8.) Partners bump a low pass to themselves and then set a high pass to their partners. This drill requires that each pair of students have as much floor space as possible to work with. Careful consideration should be given to spacing.

FIGURE 5.7   FIGURE 5.8

7. Passing line drill. (See Figure 5.9.) Students line up in two straight lines with the leaders facing each other across a net. The goal is to set the ball across the net to the opposing line player. After setting the ball, the student moves to the right and goes to the end of the other line? This drill can be made more interesting by introducing competition between two separate passing line groups (i.e., consecutive successful passes).

8. Cross-court setting drill. (See Figure 5.10.) This drill is similar to the passing line drill illustrated in Figure 5.9, except no net is involved and the ball is set from one back corner of the court to the opposite front corner of the court. The purpose of the drill is to assist the student in learning to make long and high cross-court sets to a position close to the net (spiking position). Drill is practiced from left-back to right-front and right-back to left-front.

The Basic Power Spike

The volleyball spike represents a volleyball skill that is composed of a number of subskills (approach, arm swing, vertical jump, power development, arm swing, wrist snap, and follow-through). For this reason it is considered to be a rather complex motor skill. However, if the learner already has

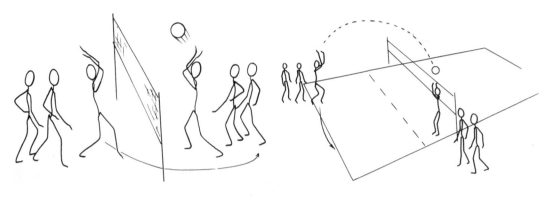

FIGURE 5.9   **FIGURE 5.10**

mastered the subskills involved in executing the spike, the actual skill of spiking can be learned quite easily (this concept is developed by Robb, 1972). If the learner, through previous experience, has learned how to jump vertically, throw a ball with opposition, and generally demonstrate good body control while in the air, he or she will likely learn how to spike rather easily. On the other hand, if the learner cannot jump vertically very well (for example), this particular subskill will demand close attention.

Execution. In executing the spike, a maximum of three to four approach steps is recommended. At the completion of the final two steps, the feet come together and the actual vertical jump is made from two feet. The spiker jumps into the air, using a double arm swing to assist in developing jumping power. Once in the air, the spiker arches the back, rotates the shoulder girdle (clockwise for right hander), and cocks the hitting arm in preparation for the spike.

In spiking the ball, abdominal muscles are contracted, shoulder girdle is rotated counterclockwise (right hander), and the ball is hit with a striking action of the open hand. As can be observed in Photo Sequence 5.4, when the ball is hit, the elbow is fully extended and the wrist joint is flexed. This wrist-flexing action of the hitting hand will impart topspin to the volleyball (see Figure 5.11).

Drills for practice. The following drills (in sequence) are suggested for use in developing skill in executing the basic power spike.

1. Floor-wall rebounding drill. (See Figure 5.12.) Learner stands 4.5 meters (about 15 ft) from a flat wall and spikes the ball into the floor so that it rebounds up onto the wall and back to the student. The student's goal is to impart topspin on the ball and to keep the ball going in a continuous cycle (floor-wall-hit). Spiker's feet do not leave the ground. Students should be spaced a minimum of 4 or 5 meters from each other in this drill.

2. Four-step-approach jumping drill. The purpose of this drill is to practice a short four-step spike approach that culminates in a double-foot vertical jump. The drill is practiced facing a flat wall to discourage long jumping. The approach involves three steps and a close-step (or hop) to bring the feet together. Students are spaced around the gym and about 3 meters (about 10 ft) from the wall.

3. Lowered-net spiking drill. Learner practices spiking the volleyball over a lowered net (lower net 30 cm or about 12 in.). For simplification, the ball is tossed (underhand and with two hands) to the spiker rather than set. The ball should be tossed about 2 meters (about 6 ft) above the net and about 60 centimeters (about 2 ft) from net. Tossing accuracy is critical.

PHOTO SEQUENCE 5.4
Technique involved in executing the basic power spike.

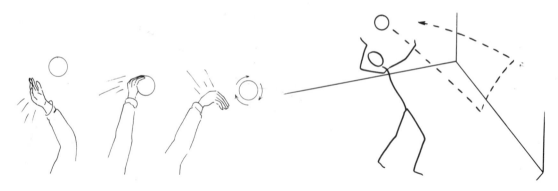

FIGURE 5.11   FIGURE 5.12

4. Setter-spiking drill. (See Figure 5.13.) Setter sets the ball to the spiker rather than tossing it (face pass). The net may be at either a lowered or regulation height. Play is initiated with the spiker tossing (or face passing) the ball to the setter. It is important to select accurate setters for the drill. Both sides of the net are utilized. After hitting, the spiker retrieves the ball and goes to the end of the other line.

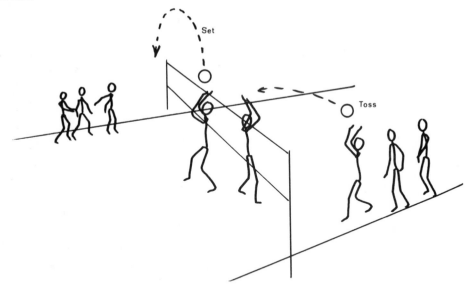

FIGURE 5.13

Individual Blocking Technique

At first glance, the act of blocking appears to be a relatively simple skill to execute and teach. Yet, it is one of the most difficult because of the precise body movements required for success. The potential importance of blocking in the modern game of volleyball cannot be overemphasized. It has been estimated that among international-level teams as many as 55 percent of the points are scored directly as a result of a block (Lowell, 1966). Blocking ranks with forearm passing (service reception) in terms of team success.

Individual blocking technique is also extremely important in terms of safety. Many volleyball injuries occur underneath the net, where poor blocking technique results in serious ankle and leg injuries. The teacher must impress upon the learner the importance of proper blocking technique for safety as well as for skillful playing.

Execution. In individual blocking technique, the blocker starts at a position within 30 centimeters (about 12 in.) of the net (see Photo Sequence 5.5). The arms should be raised and spread in anticipation of the blocking action. Fingers are spread and palms are facing the net. The blocker moves into position to oppose the spiker by using a slide-step lateral-movement technique. Once in position at the net for the block, the blocker goes into a deep crouch position. From the crouch position, the learner executes the vertical jump at a point in time slightly after the hitter has made his or her jump. As the blocker executes the vertical jump, the hands and arms glide up the net in such a fashion that no angular arm swing is involved. The blocker must not hit the bottom edge of the net during the execution of the vertical jump. This is best accomplished by eliminating any angular arm swing as well as any tendency to jump forward into the net or across the centerline.

PHOTO SEQUENCE 5.5
Student practicing individual blocking technique (ready, jump preparation, block, and recovery).

The actual blocking action is executed by extending the arms and hands above and over the net to intercept the spiked ball. As a *natural* extension of the blocking action, the wrists are flexed, and the spiked ball is deflected downward into the opponent's court. To prevent the ball from passing between the blocker's arms, the elbows should be straight and kept close together. The blocker's arms should also be close enough to the net to prevent the spiked ball from passing between the arms and the net.

After the attempted block has been effected, the blocker must withdraw the hands from the opponent's side of the net prior to floor recovery. This action will help eliminate net violations during the recovery phase of the block.

Drills for practice. The following drills (in sequence) are suggested for use in developing beginning skill in executing the individual block.

1. Stationary wall-blocking drill. Students are distributed around the gym in such a manner that they are within 30 centimeters (about 12 in.) of and facing a flat wall surface. Learners start in a ready blocking position. Upon command, the students execute a maximum vertical jump and touch block against the flat wall. A horizontal line, set at net height, should be placed on the walls as a reference marker for how high the students should jump.

2. Stationary net-blocking drill. In the net-blocking drill, three students take positions within 30 centimeters (about 12 in.) of a net. (Students should be spaced 2 meters apart.) The stationary net drill is identical to the stationary wall drill. However, the inclusion of the net makes it possible to practice arm and net relationships. It also provides important cues for eliminating foot faults and net violations.

3. Lateral movement in wall-blocking drill. (See Figure 5.14.) Learners take positions alongside walls which allow room for lateral movement. The student begins 30 centimeters (about 12 in.) from the wall and executes blocking action upon command. Upon recovery from the first jump, the student moves laterally to the left about 2.8 meters (about 9 ft) and jumps again. Upon recovery from the second jump, the learner shifts laterally to the right to the original position and jumps a third time. This procedure is done slowly at first, for technique, but later it is done very fast, for conditioning. The slide step is used for lateral movement.

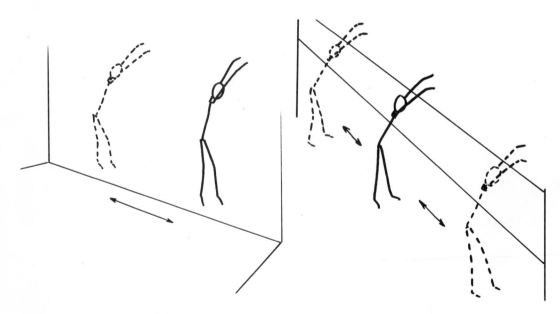

FIGURE 5.14   FIGURE 5.15

4. Lateral movement in net-blocking drill. (See Figure 5.15.) The learners take positions within 30 centimeters (about 12 in.) of the net. The net-blocking drill is very similar to the lateral-movement wall-blocking drill. The blocker, however, practices lateral slide-step movements from positions left *and* right of the center starting position. Because of limitations on net position space, both sides of the net should be utilized. Each student takes ten jumps before the next person in line steps in.

5. Group blocking drill with opposing partner. (See Figure 5.16.) Six students pair off facing each other at three positions along the net (left, center, and right). Upon command, the opposing blockers execute simultaneous blocks at the net. In doing this, they clap hands over the net, being careful not to foot fault or touch the net. Upon recovery, the blockers shift to the next position on the net and execute the next jump and block (upon command). After jumping from each of three positions, the blockers go to the end of the opposing line. This is a good drill for conditioning as well as for technique.

6. Individual blocking against a spike. (See Figure 5.17.) The purpose of this drill is to give the student practice at blocking a spiked ball. Each blocker gets five consecutive chances to block a spike. The spikers, however, chase their hit and get into the end of the line after each spike. Every spiker should receive a turn at blocking. Drill groups (4 to 6 students) may be formed at the two on-hand (right side) positions of the net.

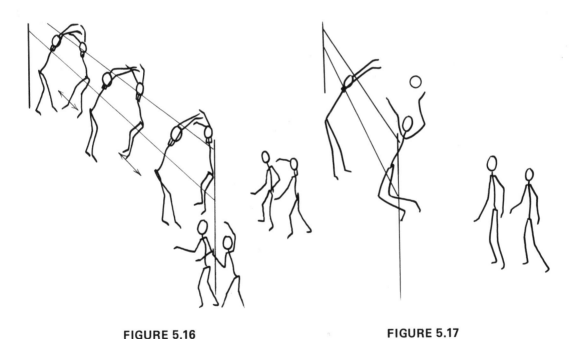

FIGURE 5.16   **FIGURE 5.17**

Tandem Blocking Technique

While a blocker is often forced to try to block a spike alone, the best blocking situation will involve at least two people. Consequently, it would be desirable from a defensive point of view to execute a tandem block on every attack situation. However, the very act of effecting a double block cannot assure success. That is, the ability of two blockers to work in unison is crucial. It may be better from a defensive point of view to have a single block rather than a poor double block. This is because a bad block can often do for the spiker what the spiker cannot do for himself: score a point.

Execution. In executing the tandem block, the outside blocker generally has the responsibility of "setting" the block. In "setting" the block, the outside blocker establishes a stable position directly opposite the approaching spiker. The middle blocker has the responsibility of moving rapidly into a position tandem (side by side) to the outside blocker. It is important in executing the tandem block that the blockers jump in unison and demonstrate good individual blocking technique. The execution of the tandem block is illustrated in Photo Sequence 5.6.

Drills for practice. The following drills (in sequence) are suggested for use in developing skill in executing the tandem block.

1. Tandem blocking drill without spike. (See Figure 5.18.) Three blockers take blocking positions at the net (left, middle, and right). On the opposite side of the net are the instructor (in center of court) and two assistants (students) in on- and off-hand positions close to the net. When the instructor (or student) throws the ball to one of the assistants at the net, the line blocker (opposite the ball) and the middle blocker converge for a tandem block. The blockers jump in unison when the assistant tosses the ball (underhand) into the air above the net. After the blockers attempt to block the ball, they return to their starting positions. This continues until the middle blocker has attempted ten blocks (5 in each direction). New blockers rotate into position.

2. Tandem blocking drill against nondeceptive spikers. (See Figure 5.19.) This drill is similar to drill 1, except that the ball is actually spiked rather than merely tossed. When the ball is set to the spiker, the blockers converge for a tandem block. To make sure the blockers get blocking practice, the spiker makes no attempt to deceive the blockers, but spikes the ball into the hands of the blockers. The spikers that are selected for the drill should be able to spike with control. Two spikers are used in the drill (at one time). One attacks from the on-hand position, the other from the off-hand. The two spikers receive sets in an alternating fashion (no deception), so that the blockers know in advance which spiker will spike the ball.

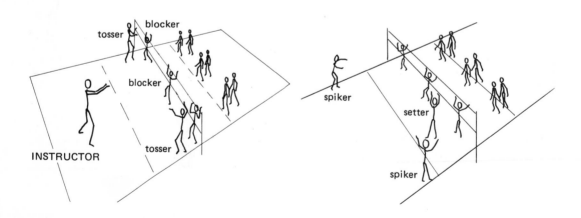

FIGURE 5.18   **FIGURE 5.19**

PHOTO SEQUENCE 5.6

Outside and middle blockers executing a tandem block against an on-hand hitter. Picture reproduced with permission from K. Herzog, *Volleyball Movements in Photographic Sequence* (Ottawa, Ontario: Canadian Volleyball Association, 1976).

FIGURE 5.20

3. Tandem blocking drill against deceptive spikers. (See Figure 5.20.) This drill is like drill 2, except that both the setter and the spikers become deceptive. The setter randomly sets the on- and off-hand spike. Since this involves backsetting, the instructor or skilled student does the setting. Also, the spikers do not purposely try to spike the ball into the block. As in the other two drills, the blockers take a turn blocking at a particular blocking position and rotate to the end of a line for the next position. Generally, a blocker should make about five block attempts per position before rotating out.

EXECUTION AND TEACHING TEAM STRATEGIES OF PLAY

Certain concepts of team play should be taught to beginners: (a) W-receiving formation for offense, (b) simple 3-deep defense, and (c) transition from defense to offense (free ball) and vice versa. Mastery of these concepts is as critical to beginning volleyball as development of individual skills. Each concept will be discussed in terms of its execution and a sequence of suggested learning experiences.

The W-Receiving Formation

The W-receiving formation represents the foundation of the offensive system used by the beginner. The team receiving the serve is said to be the offensive team. It is their goal to attack the opposition, using the skills of bumping, setting, and spiking.

Execution. The W-formation is illustrated in Figure 5.21*b*. Figure 5.21*a* shows the relative rotational positions of all six players prior to assuming the W-formation. The W-formation observed here is the same as the one diagrammed in Figure 5.6 for team receiving practice. In the W-formation in Figure 5.21, the middle front player is the setter. Each time the team rotates, a new player becomes the middle front player and also the setter. The left front player (LF) is the on-hand spiker, and the right front player (RF) is the off-hand hitter. It is the responsibility of the players in the W-formation to pass the ball to the setter (MF), who sets the ball to either the on-hand or off-hand spiker.

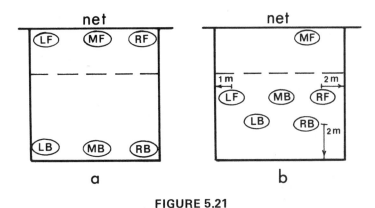

FIGURE 5.21

In the W-formation, the three front-line receivers (LF, MB, and RF) take short serves that would otherwise drop in front of them. All other serves (deep serves) are the responsibility of the two primary receivers (LB and RB). The primary receivers should back up all serves and personally receive 80 percent of them. The setter (MF) assumes a ready position to the right of center when waiting for the bump. The setter faces the on-hand hitter (LF). From this position most bumped balls will be in front of the setter (backpeddling is difficult). In a beginning class, the majority of the sets should be set to the on-hand spiker (LF).

Finally, it is important in team receiving formations that players practice calling the ball. If a ball is coming to the left back receiver (LB), he or she should call "mine" or "I got it." It is also important that players become physically aggressive when they call a ball (Peppler, 1977). This lets teammates know that the person calling the ball is actually going to take it.

Suggested learning experiences. The following demonstrations and lead-up game experiences will help the student understand the W-formation.

1. Using a group of team captains, demonstrate the W-receiving formation to the class. Go through an entire six-person rotation, showing how team members drop back into W-formation from each rotation. Discuss area receiving responsibilities and answer questions.

2. The above demonstration is repeated on each individual court, with the group and team members being the participants, and the group leaders (captains) doing the directing. The instructor should assist where needed but should not dominate the instruction. This will allow the learners and the group leaders the opportunity to answer many of their own questions.

3. Students next practice the W-formation in a lead-up game situation. Players take their positions on the court. Both teams assume W-formations. The team serving the ball will serve five balls in

succession. After each serve, the ball is played until it is dead. Regardless of which side wins a "point," the same team continues to serve. After the five serves, both teams rotate one position. The same team that served before, serves another five times. This continues until the serving team has served 30 balls. After 30 serves by one team, the other team becomes the serving team and serves 30 times. Served balls that hit the net or go out of bounds do not count.

4. Teams practice the W-formation in a game situation. Instructor and/or team captains should stop play to make corrective adjustments in the W-formation when necessary.

The 3-Deep Defense

As the students master the W-receiving formation and become successful in the offensive phase of the game (bump, set, and spike), it should become apparent to all that some sort of team defense is necessary. For the beginning level, the team defense selected should be simple to learn and execute. The 3-deep defense is therefore ideal.

Execution. The initial phase of all defensive systems is known as the spread formation. From the spread formation, the defensive team shifts into the 3-deep defense. The nature of this shift depends on the opponents' attack. The spread formation for the 3-deep defense is illustrated in Figure 5.22a. A team assumes the defensive spread formation when they are certain the opposition is going to be on offense. At this point the defensive team does not know which member of the attacking team will spike the ball. Consequently, when the defensive team is in the spread formation, all front line players assume blocking positions near the net. Conversely, the back-row players play deep, with the exception of the middle back player. The middle back player assumes a position on or close to the 3-meter (about 10-ft) line.

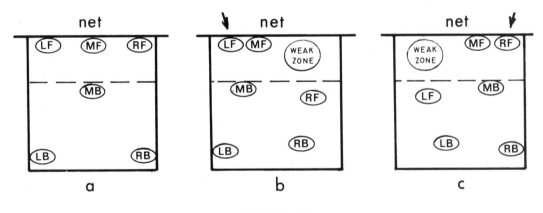

FIGURE 5.22

When the ball is actually set to a spiker on the offensive side of the net, the defense shifts accordingly. If the offense sets their off-hand hitter, the defense shifts as illustrated in Figure 5.22b. If the on-hand hitter is set, the defense shifts as illustrated in Figure 5.22c. In executing the 3-deep defense, each member of the team has specific responsibilities to carry out. Using Figure 5.22c as the example, the players have the following assignments. The middle front (MF) and right front (RF) players block the ball. Since the left front (LF) player is not blocking, he or she drops back behind the 3-meter line to dig the spike. The left back (LB) and right back (RB) players try to dig spikes that are hit into their areas. The middle back (MB) player plays right behind the block and tries to get easy balls passing just over the block. Specifics of player position responsibilities for the 3-deep defense are listed in Table 5.1.

TABLE 5.1
PLAYER POSITION RESPONSIBILITIES FOR THE 3-DEEP DEFENSE*

POSITION	RESPONSIBILITIES
Middle Front and Right Front (MF & RF)	Block.
Right Back (RB)	Spikes hit down the line.
Middle Back (MB)	Soft spikes hit short and over the block.
Left Back (LB)	Deep spikes over block. Cover entire baseline for spike deflecting off block.
Left Front (LF)	Hard cross-court spikes.

*Refer to Figure 5.22c.

Suggested learning experiences. The following demonstrations and lead-up game experiences will help the student understand the 3-deep defense:

1. Using group or team captains, demonstrate the 3-deep defense to the class.

2. The above demonstration is repeated on each individual court, with the group and team members being the participants and the group leaders (captains) doing the directing.

3. Students next practice the 3-deep defense in a lead-up game situation. Players take positions on the court. The team practicing defense (Team A) assumes a defensive spread formation (Figure 5.22a). Team A will be serving the ball. Team B is the receiving team. The receiving team (Team B) assumes a W-receiving formation (Figure 5.21b). Team B practices the offensive phase of the game (bump, set, spike), while Team A practices defense. Team A serves five easy serves in succession from each rotation. This continues until each member of Team A has served five balls (balls served into net or out of bounds are re-served). When the serving team (Team A) has served 30 times, the two teams switch roles. Team B practices defense, and Team A practices offense. In this lead-up game, the receiving team rotates when the serving team does. Also, the ball becomes dead after the ball has been spiked (do not rally for point).

4. Normally, the teams would now practice the new team concepts in a controlled game situation. In this case, however, this should not be attempted until the concept of team defense-offense transition has been taught.

Defense-Offense Transition

The notion that a team makes some sort of dynamic transition when going from offense to defense (or vice versa) in such sports as basketball, soccer, and football is well accepted. However, this idea is not at all apparent to the novice volleyball player. This concept must be taught to the beginner, since the team offense and defense cannot function effectively without it.

Execution. A team starts every play in either an offensive or a defensive posture. For example, the serving team (Team B) is on offense (W-formation). However, once a rally begins, the two teams are continually changing roles. As soon as Team B hits the ball across the net, they must assume a defensive posture. Conversely, Team A must go on the offensive. These two situations require that both teams be continually shifting back and forth from a defensive spread formation to a W-receiving formation.

The transitional situations that transpire during the course of a rally are illustrated in Figure 5.23. The defensive spread formation is depicted in Figure 5.23a. A team (Team A) assumes this formation when they serve and immediately after spiking a ball across the net (transition from c to a). When Team A is on defense, one of two things generally occurs. First, Team A may be required to defend against a spike as in Figure 5.23b (transition from a to b); or second, Team A may drop back into an offensive W-formation (transition from a to c). This situation occurs when the offensive team (Team B) does not spike the ball, but merely bumps or sets it back. When this occurs, Team A drops back quickly into the W-receiving formation for offense. This event is called a *free ball,* since Team A gets an easy ball back from the opponents rather than a spike. Conversely, the team that starts on offense (Team B) must be prepared to go on defense as soon as they volley the ball across the net (transition from c to a).

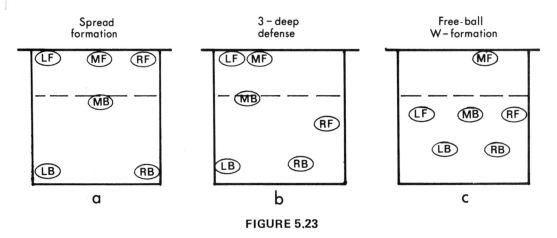

FIGURE 5.23

Suggested learning experiences. The following demonstrations and lead-up game experiences will help the student understand the notion of team transition from defense to offense and vice versa.

1. Using group or team captains, demonstrate team transition from defense to offense and offense to defense to the class. The information illustrated in Figure 5.23 will be the basis of this discussion and demonstration.

2. The above demonstration is repeated on each individual court, with the group and team members being the participants and the group leaders (captains) doing the directing.

3. Students next practice the 3-deep defense and W-receiving formation in a lead-up game situation. Team A is first designated as the serving team (defensive team), and Team B as the receiving team (offensive team). Team A assumes a defensive spread formation as depicted in Figure 5.23a and

serves five times from each rotational position. After every member of Team A has served five balls each (30 serves in all), the two teams changes roles. The serving team (Team A) becomes the receivers, and the receiving team (Team B) the servers. In executing the drill, the ball continues in play after every serve until it becomes dead. Both teams will thus be involved in numerous transitional situations. The serving team, for example, will go from a defensive spread formation to a W-formation whenever the receiving team makes a bad pass. With beginners this will happen on as many as 60 percent of all serves.

4. Teams practice the transition aspects of offense and defense in a game situation. Instructor and/or team captains should make corrective adjustments when necessary.

SUGGESTED STUDENT PROJECTS

1. The information in this chapter makes no distinction in teaching beginning volleyball to different age groups. Consider what adaptations you might make in teaching (a) children ages 9 to 12, (b) young people ages 13 to 15, (c) young adults ages 16 to 18, and (d) adults.

2. Prepare a bulletin-board display showing the W-receiving formation in terms of (a) spatial relationships between players, (b) spatial relationships between players, net, and sidelines (use metric system), and (c) positional responsibilities.

3. Prepare a bulletin-board display showing the 3-deep defense in terms of court positions and player responsibilities for (a) an on-hand attack and (b) an off-hand attack.

4. Research several volleyball books, or use your imagination, to design (on paper) three volleyball drills—involving 6 to 10 players—for practicing the skills of forearm passing and face passing.

5. Prepare a 20-question true-false test from the rules listed in Box 5.1. In addition, compose a 20-question multiple-choice test on the skills and team strategies discussed in chapter 5.

REFERENCES

Herzog, K. *Volleyball Movements in Photographic Sequence.* Ottawa, Ontario: Canadian Volleyball Association, 1976.

Peppler, M.J. *Inside Volleyball for Women.* Chicago: Henry Regnery Co., 1977.

Robb, M.D. *The Dynamics of Motor Skill Acquisition.* Englewood Cliffs, New Jersey: Prentice-Hall, Inc., 1972, pp. 42-50.

Lowell, J.C. "International Blocking: An Offensive Weapon." *International Volleyball Review,* 24 (1966), 8-9.

6

Volleyball Instruction for Intermediate Performers

This chapter on teaching volleyball to intermediate-level students is patterned after the organizational format of chapter 5. Specifically, section one will be composed of a sample teaching progression of 30 or 20 micro-units; section two will elaborate on the techniques of teaching the fundamental skills introduced in the progression; and section three will discuss the execution and teaching of team strategies of play.

Since the skills and strategies taught to beginners will need to be reviewed for the students in the intermediate class, the teacher must be familiar with the material in chapter 5. Many of the drills and lead-up game experiences discussed in relationship to beginners will be applicable for the instruction of intermediate-level learners as well. The several skills and team strategies that will be discussed in this chapter come from those outlined in the progressions.

SAMPLE TEACHING PROGRESSION

As in chapter 5, the progression for intermediate students is composed of 30 micro-units of instruction. By eliminating the micro-units that are marked with an asterisk (*), the progression may be shortened to 20 micro-units (days).

Micro-Unit 1. Class organization
    a. Introductions.
    b. Attendance and grading procedures.
    c. Required wearing apparel, shower and locker room procedures.
    d. Instruction on set-up and take-down of nets.
    e. Explain roll call procedures.

*Micro-Unit 2. Testing and organization
    a. Pre-testing on the following skill tests.
        (1) Brumbach forearm passing wall-volley test.
        (2) AAHPER face passing wall-volley test.
    b. Use skill test scores to organize class into homogeneous team groupings.

Micro-Unit 3. Review rules and play volleyball
    a. Distribute rules handout from chapter 5 (Box 5.1).

    b. Expand upon rule 19 of Box 5.1. (Note: Since switching of positions, as involved in the 4-2 offense, will be taught in this chapter, the concept of overlapping must be clearly understood.)

        (1) All players must be in relative serving order at the instant the ball is served.

        (2) Overlaps can only occur with adjacent players on different rows (left-front and left-back) or with adjacent players on same row (left-front and center-front).

        (3) The NFSHSA (1978-79) rules state that "no part of one player's body touching the floor shall overlap any part of another player's body touching the floor."

        (4) USVBA (1979) rules are more liberal than the NFSHA rules. They state that "at the moment the ball is served, the backline players must be at least a little behind their corresponding frontline players."

    c. Play volleyball for the purpose of observing general knowledge and skill level of students.

Micro-Unit 4. The overhand floating serve

    a. Discussion.

    b. Demonstration.

    c. Drills for practice.

    d. Utilize overhand floating serve in game situation.

*Micro-Unit 5. Review W-receiving formation and 3-deep defense

    a. Discussion of team play.

    b. Demonstrations.

    c. If necessary, practice selected learning experiences from chapter 5.

    d. Utilize W-formation and 3-deep defense in game situation.

Micro-Unit 6. Review forearm pass for receiving and face pass for forward set

    a. Discussion.

    b. Demonstration.

    c. If necessary, practice selected drills from chapter 5.

    d. Utilize forearm pass and front set in game situation.

Micro-Unit 7. Teach the back set using the face pass

    a. Discussion.

    b. Demonstration.

    c. Drills for practice.

    d. Utilize back set in game situation.

*Micro-Unit 8. Review the basic power spike

    a. Discussion.

    b. Demonstration.

    c. If necessary, practice selected spiking drills from chapter 5.

    d. Utilize volleyball spike in game situation.

Micro-Unit 9. Teach cross-court and down-the-line spiking

    a. Discussion.

    b. Demonstration.

    c. Drills for practice.

    d. Utilize in game situation.

*Micro-Unit 10. Review cross-court and down-the-line spiking
   a. Discussion.
   b. Drills for practice.
   c. Utilize in game situation.

Micro-Unit 11. Review individual and tandem blocking technique
   a. Discussion.
   b. Demonstration.
   c. If necessary, practice selected blocking drills from chapter 5.
   d. Utilize individual and tandem blocking in game situation.

*Micro-Unit 12. Teach the Japanese roll
   a. Discussion.
   b. Demonstration.
   c. Drills for practice.
   d. Play volleyball.

Micro-Unit 13. Teach the Japanese roll for the one-arm dig.
   a. Discussion.
   b. Demonstration.
   c. Drills for practice.
   d. Utilize Japanese roll and one-arm dig in game situation.

Micro-Unit 14. Teach the Japanese roll for digging (forearm pass) and setting
   a. Discussion.
   b. Demonstration.
   c. Drills for practice.
   d. Utilize Japanese roll for digging and setting in game situation.

Micro-Unit 15. Teach the 4-deep defense.
   a. Discussion.
   b. Demonstration.
   c. Learning experiences for practice.

Micro-Unit 16. Teach defense-to-offense free-ball transition
   a. Discussion.
   b. Demonstration.
   c. Learning experiences for practice.
   d. Utilize the 4-deep defense in game situation.

Micro-Unit 17. Teach the concept of switching positions and the 4-2 offense
   a. Discussion.
   b. Demonstration.
   c. Learning experiences for practice.

*Micro-Unit 18. Testing and review
   a. Administer short true-false test on rules.
   b. Review skills and team tactics taught.

Micro-Unit 19. Teach spike coverage for the 4-2 offense
   a. Discussion.
   b. Demonstration.
   c. Learning experiences for practice.
   d. Utilize spike coverage in game situation.

*Micro-Unit 20. Play volleyball
   a. Instructor serves as a referee for 10 minutes on each court.
   b. Instructor looks for weaknesses in skill and team strategy.

*Micro-Unit 21. Review and provide mini-units of instruction on weak areas identified in Micro-Unit 20

*Micro-Unit 22. Intra-class volleyball tournament

*Micro-Unit 23. Intra-class volleyball tournament

Micro-Unit 24. Intra-class volleyball tournament

Micro-Unit 25. Intra-class volleyball tournament

Micro-Unit 26. Intra-class volleyball tournament

Micro-Unit 27. Intra-class volleyball tournament

Micro-Unit 28. Volleyball skill testing (See chapter 8, Evaluation)

*Micro-Unit 29. Physical fitness testing (See chapter 8, Evaluation)

Micro-Unit 30. Written examination on skill and team strategy techniques discussed during unit of instruction.

TEACHING THE FUNDAMENTAL SKILLS

Each of the fundamental skills covered in this section will be discussed in terms of execution and drills for practice. The teacher is reminded that appropriate drills may be selected from those provided.

The Overhand Floating Serve

The intermediate-level volleyball player should be ready to learn the overhand floating serve. The overhand floating serve is by far the most common method of serving in the United States (at all levels of play). Like the underhand floater, it is easy to control, yet it is difficult to receive because of its unpredictable flight pattern. The fact that it is served from above the head rather than from an underhand position enhances its offensive potential.

Execution. The execution of the overhand floating serve is illustrated in Photo Sequence 6.1. As shown in the photo sequence, the ball is tossed without spin about 1 meter (about 3 ft) above the head. As the server steps forward (or shifts weight) with the lead leg (leg opposite hitting arm), the striking arm is cocked back in a hitting position. The ball is contacted at full extension of the arm directly over the head and slightly in front of the body. The ball is contacted in the center of its axis by the heel of the striking hand (hand is open). The ball is hit firmly, but with little follow-through. The entire serving action is similar to the shoulder action used in throwing a softball or football.

PHOTO SEQUENCE 6.1
Execution of the overhand floating serve.

Drills for practice. The suggested drills for learning the overhand floating serve are identical to those given for the underhand floating serve in chapter 5.

The Back Set

The back set is included in the intermediate progression for purposes of offensive deception. If it were not for the objective of deception, it would be simpler to make forward sets to both on- and off-hand spikers by turning the face to the spiker. Deception, however, adds a new and exciting aspect to the game of volleyball. When a setter can set forward and backward with equal skill, the defense must wait until the last split second before forming a tandem block.

Execution. The initial phase of the face pass for back setting is identical to the forward set (see chapter 5, pp. 33-34). But instead of setting the ball up and forward, the ball is set up and backwards. This skill technique is illustrated in Photo Sequence 6.2. As can be observed, the setter moves into a crouch position underneath the ball. The arms and hands are raised above the head in readiness for the set. The legs are in stride position, and the ball is directly above the face. As the ball is set, the back is arched and the head is extended backwards. The ball contacts the setter's hands on the inside pads of the fingers and thumbs (distal phalanges). The ball is actually "set" backwards rather than forward (it is not deflected backwards).

Drills for practice. The following drills (in sequence) are suggested for use in developing skill in executing the back set face pass.

1. Wall drill for two people. (See Figure 6.1.) Two students utilize a wall (as the third person) to practice back setting. One student stands with back to a flat wall (2 meters away from the wall). The other student faces the former with a distance of 4 meters (about 13 ft) separating them. The

PHOTO SEQUENCE 6.2
Execution of the back set using the face pass.

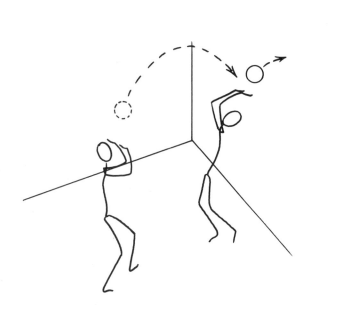

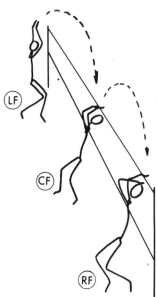

FIGURE 6.1   FIGURE 6.2

student farthest from the wall face passes the ball to the student with back to the wall. This student, in turn, back sets the ball into the wall (aiming at a point 4 meters above the floor). The ball will rebound off the wall to the student facing the wall, who either continues the volley or catches the ball.

2. Back setting drill for two people. Two students face each other with a distance of 4 meters (about 13 ft) separating them. When the ball is volleyed to player A, player A volleys the ball to himself or herself (about 2 meters above the head), makes a 180-degree turn, and back sets the ball to his or her partner, player B. This drill is also very good for practicing side sets and regular front sets.

3. Back setting drill for three people. (See Figure 6.2.) Three students take positions by a net, against a wall or on a line marked on the floor. If an actual net is available for each group of six students (three per side), they line up as follows. Two students face each other with a distance of 9 meters (about 30 ft) separating them (standing on court sidelines about 1 meter from the net). The third student takes a position between the first two, with the right side of his or her body to the net. The student standing in the left front (LF) position at the net initiates play by volleying the ball to the center front (CF) player. The center front player back sets to the right front (RF) player, who in turn makes a long cross-court set to the left front player. Players rotate positions after twenty back setting attempts.

4. Back setting lead-up game drill for four people. (See Figure 6.3.) In this drill, a phase of the actual game is simulated by including a forearm passer in the back setting drill. The left front (LF) player tosses the ball to the receiver (R) who forearm passes the ball to the setter (CF). The setter back sets to the right front (RF) player, who in turn makes a cross-court set to the left front player. After each player has made 20-25 plays at one position, all four players rotate clockwise one position.

5. Back setting drill to a spiker. (See Figure 6.4.) The setter practices front and back sets to spikers. The setter alternates setting the ball to the on-hand (front set) and off-hand (back set) spikers.

FIGURE 6.3   **FIGURE 6.4**

The balls are passed to the setter by the instructor or a designated student. Setters should make 10 to 15 back sets before a new setter rotates in. After spiking the ball, the spiker chases the ball and goes to the end of the other spiking line.

Directional Spiking

The beginner has been taught to spike the ball into the center of the court. Mastery of this skill is essential to the development of a volleyball player. However, as the beginner is confronted with better and more effective tandem-blocking teams, his spiking effectiveness begins to decline. This is because a ball that is spiked towards the center of the court will generally be intercepted by the tandem block. For this reason, the intermediate-level volleyball player must learn to hit the "angles." Hitting the angles means that the spiker must be able to spike the ball in three directions. As depicted in Figure 6.5, these are the cross-court spike, the center-of-the-court spike, and the down-the-line spike.

Execution. As illustrated in Figure 6.5, the on-hand hitter approaches the net at an angle in line with a center-of-the-court spike. Consequently, the same approach angle is used regardless of the intended direction of the spike. This technique tends to keep the tandem block from setting up on the spiker's intended spike angle. With highly skilled volleyball players, the decision to spike the ball down-the-line or cross-court does not take place until the spiker is in the air. This decision is based partly on the nature and position of the block, and on the nature and position of the set ball. To hit the ball down-the-line, the spiker must allow the ball to pass in front of his or her body. Conversely, to hit the ball cross-court, the spiker attacks the ball before it crosses in front of his or her body. These same principles apply for the off-hand spike. In the off-hand spike, however, the approach angle is different. The off-hand spiker approaches the net at an angle in line with a down-the-line spike. This description, as well as Figure 6.5, assumes a right-handed spiker.

Drills for practice. Since many of the drills recommended for learning directional spiking are similar to those encountered in the basic power spike, the reader is referred to the spiking section of chapter 5 (pp. 35-38). The following drills are specifically suggested for use in learning to spike cross-court and down-the-line.

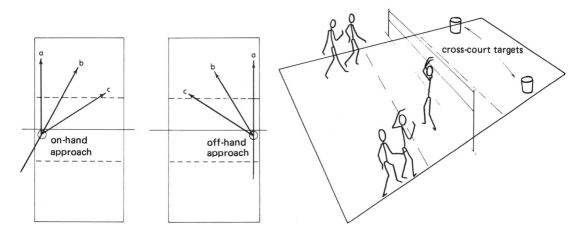

FIGURE 6.5   **FIGURE 6.6**

1. **Cross-court spiking target drill.** (See Figure 6.6.) The spikers form hitting lines as illustrated in Figure 6.4. The setter alternates setting the ball to on-hand and off-hand hitters. The spikers must attempt to hit targets that are set in cross-court spiking positions. After spiking the ball, the hitter chases his or her ball and gets into the end of the other line. Folding chairs, plastic wastepaper baskets, and cardboard boxes are all ideal for targets.

2. **Down-the-line spiking target drill.** This drill is identical to the one illustrated in Figure 6.6, except that the targets are used for down-the-line spiking. Two interesting innovations of the target-spiking drills are (a) use real diggers for targets, and (b) organize hitting lines as depicted in Figure 5.13 of chapter 5.

3. **Cross-court spiking drill with blocker and digger.** (See Figure 6.7.) This drill is very similar to the drill depicted in Figure 6.6, except that cross-court diggers and down-the-line blockers are employed. The diggers dig the spikes and serve as targets. The blockers, however, merely encourage the cross-court spike by blocking a down-the-line attack. After spiking, a hitter becomes a blocker and the blocker becomes a digger. Diggers retrieve the spiked balls and go to the end of the other line.

4. **Down-the-line spiking drill with blocker and digger.** This drill is identical to the drill depicted in Figure 6.7, except that the spikers hit the ball down-the-line. The diggers dig down-the-line spikes and serve as targets. The blockers encourage down-the-line spikes by closing off the cross-court angle. As in drill 3, the spikers become blockers, blockers become diggers, and diggers become spikers after each spike attempt.

5. **Angle spiking against tandem blocking.** (See Figure 6.8.) In this drill, three blockers are employed. The middle blocker and a line blocker form a tandem block against on- and off-hand spike attacks. The spikers attempt to avoid being blocked by hitting cross-court or down-the-line. Back-court diggers dig both cross-court and down-the-line spikes from the two spiking lines. For rotational purposes, defensive players (blockers and diggers) switch roles with offensive players (spikers and setter) after spikers have had at least five spike attempts from each line.

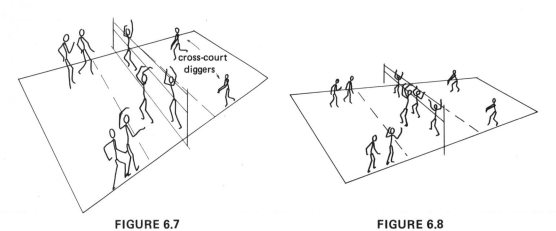

cross-court diggers

FIGURE 6.7   **FIGURE 6.8**

The Japanese Roll

One of the most exciting aspects of volleyball play is that which takes place in the backcourt when a team is on defense. While most offensive spikes are defended via the block or the forearm pass "dig," it is often necessary for an individual to make a diving or rolling attempt to field a difficult spike. Defensively speaking, each member of the backcourt has a specific area or zone to cover. However, to cover this assigned area it sometimes becomes necessary to make an all-out effort for a ball.

As a means for extending one's range of defensive effectiveness, the Japanese roll and forward dive (to be introduced in chapter 7) should be considered safety skills. Some educators have pointed out the dangers inherent in executing a diving or rolling save and have discouraged their inclusion in instructional programs. Their argument is that such tactics can only be mastered effectively by skilled athletes in highly organized athletic programs. There is some merit to this position, yet when the skills are viewed as safety skills, then an opposing position must be taken. For example, what is to stop the novice from attempting a "not-so-safe" diving try for a game saver? In fact, this is exactly what happens in many cases. A student gets emotionally involved in a game and makes a desperate try at a ball that might make the difference between winning and losing. However, not having any training in the proper safety techniques for executing a sideward roll, the student falls awkwardly and is injured. In reality, the Japanese roll is a safe way to fall down and get up quickly.

The basic components of the Japanese roll are used as a means to get into position for three kinds of plays. First, the setter may use the Japanese roll (or components of it) to make an otherwise impossible set (Photo Sequence 6.3a). Backcourt defensive players often use components of the Japanese roll to get under and "dig" hard-driven spikes (Photo Sequence 6.3b). Finally, backcourt players often use a one-arm "dig" and full Japanese roll to make plays on balls that cannot be reached with a face pass or forearm pass (see Photo Sequence 6.3c).

a   b   c

PHOTO SEQUENCE 6.3
The initial phase of the Japanese roll in conjunction with the set, the forearm pass,
and the one-arm dig.

Execution. Since the set and forearm pass have been discussed in other sections of chapters 5 and 6, the execution of the Japanese roll will be described here in terms of the one-arm "dig." In executing the one-arm "dig" and the Japanese roll, six basic components may be identified. They are described and illustrated on the next page in Photo Sequence 6.4.

1. The athlete makes an initial long step in the direction of the expected interception point of the ball. If this is to the individual's right, the initial step is with the right leg towards the right.

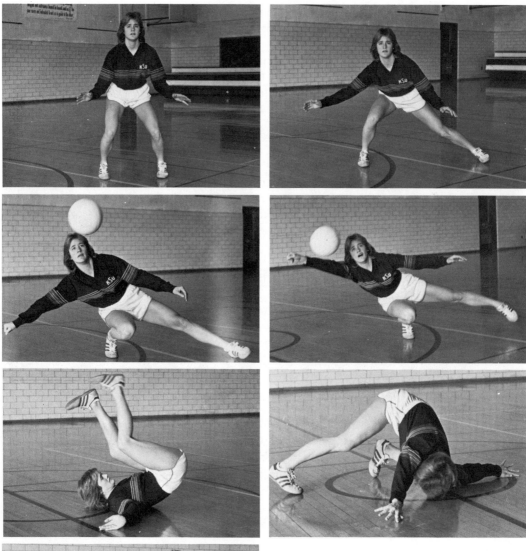

PHOTO SEQUENCE 6.4
Execution of the Japanese roll and one-arm dig.

2. The individual bends (flexes) the knee joint of the lead leg at the same time the trail leg is extended. This dual action places the athlete's buttocks within 30 centimeters (about 12 in.) of the floor.

3. Simultaneously with 2 above, the upper trunk is rotated clockwise about the hips. This allows the striking arm to be extended and readied for a striking action. At this point, the hand is positioned for striking the ball. While either a clenched fist or an open hand can be used, the main thing is to keep the elbow extended (straight) and attempt to contact the ball with the heel of the hand. If the elbow and hand are relatively straight, a ball could be played accurately anywhere along the extended arm.

4. In actually striking the ball, the upper trunk is rotated counterclockwise (right-handed dig), the body is extended at the hips, and a forward striking motion is made (horizontal flexion) with the extended right arm. In executing this action, the ball should be contacted first, followed by body contact with the floor. The buttocks contact the floor first, followed by the lower back and shoulders. This floor contact should not be painful, since the initial fall is only 30 centimeters (about 12 in.) and is taken on the best-padded part of the anatomy.

5. The next thing to consider in the sideward roll—after the ball is contacted—is the actual roll. This part of the Japanese roll is a follow-through motion and is not strictly necessary, since the athlete could merely rock forward again to regain the feet. However, the roll, as a follow-through action, is recommended as an integral part of the Japanese roll due to its simplicity and speed of recovery. In executing the roll, the student merely tucks the head to the side of the hitting arm and rolls directly backwards and over the shoulder of the nonhitting arm. The nonhitting arm should be straight and in full contact with the floor surface to avoid a barrel roll (rolling lengthwise).

6. After the roll is completed, the student regains his feet by pushing up with the hands. If the student is wearing knee guards, knee contact with the floor can be helpful. However, if knee guards are not worn, knee contact can be avoided by making early toe and ball-of-the-foot contact with the floor after completion of the roll.

Drills for practice. The following drills (in sequence) are suggested for use in developing skill in executing the Japanese roll. In all of these drills, it is suggested that students wear long-sleeved sweat tops and pants to avoid unnecessary scrapes and bruises.

1. **Group practice without a ball.** (See Figure 6.9.) The instructor leads the entire class through a step-by-step progression of the Japanese roll. The steps as described in the execution section should be followed in slow motion. The drill should continue until all students can execute the roll with confidence in either a left or right direction. The class members should be spread out over the entire gym area, allowing room for each student to move laterally. If a large wrestling mat is available, the drill may begin on the softer surface first and move to the gym floor later.

2. **Small-group instruction without ball.** The students break up into small groups of approximately six per group. The students practice the Japanese roll with assistance from a skilled group member (assign a skilled student to each group, if possible). The instructor rotates between groups and provides assistance where needed. Students should gain confidence in the basic Japanese roll before trying the next drill. Again, some students may benefit from practice on a wrestling mat.

3. **Practicing in pairs with a ball.** Students work in pairs and take turns tossing ten balls underhand to the sides of their partners (alternating left and right). The students stand 2 meters (about 7 ft) apart and toss the ball about 2 meters to the side of the receiver's position. At the apex of the toss, the ball should be 1 meter (about 3 ft) above the floor. The receiver executes the roll laterally (hits ball to partner), and immediately prepares for a roll to the other side. Pairs of students should be distributed a safe distance from each other. A wrestling mat may be used if availalbe.

FIGURE 6.9   **FIGURE 6.10**

4. Pepper drill with ball. (See Figure 6.10.) Two students stand about 3 meters apart (about 10 ft) and spike the ball at each other. The spiker (without jumping) hits balls at the receiver in such a manner that he or she must use the Japanese roll and other defensive techniques to field the ball. The digger attempts to volley the ball back to the spiker so that the drill is continuous.

EXECUTION AND TEACHING TEAM STRATEGIES OF PLAY

In addition to a review of the team concepts of play for beginners (W-receiving formation, 3-deep defense, and free-ball transition), the intermediate class should be taught several new team strategies. These strategies are (a) the 4-deep defense, (b) transition from defense to offense, (c) the 4-2 offense, and (d) spike coverage. Each of these new team strategies will be discussed in terms of execution and suggested learning experiences.

The 4-Deep Defense

The 4-deep defense (also called middle-back or man-back) is easily the most popular defensive system used by organized volleyball teams in the United States. The 4-deep defense is especially effective against power hitting teams that do not resort to many off-speed spikes. This is because it allows four players to be positioned in the backcourt for digging hard spikes. The vulnerability of the defense lies in the fact that the individuals responsible for covering soft spikes (dinks over the block) are also responsible for digging hard spikes in their area.

Execution. As indicated in chapter 5, the initial phase of all defensive systems is known as the spread formation. The spread formation for the 4-deep defense is illustrated in Figure 6.11a. A team assumes the spread formation when they are certain the opposition is going to be on offense. At this point in time, it is not known which member of the attacking team will spike the ball.

The spread formation of the 4-deep defense is identical to the spread formation of the 3-deep defense, with the exception of the position of the middle back-row player. In the 4-deep defense, the center back player begins in a position 3 meters (about 10 ft) forward of the baseline. From this position, the middle back (MB) player can react to balls that are hit across the net on the first or second touch by the opponents.

When the ball is actually set to a spiker on the offensive side of the net (Team B), the defense (Team A) shifts accordingly. If Team B sets their off-hand spiker, the defense (Team A) shifts as

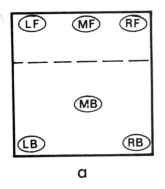

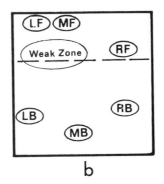

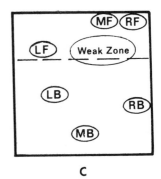

a   b   c

FIGURE 6.11

illustrated in Figure 6.11c. In executing the 4-deep defense, each member of Team A has specific responsibilities to carry out. Using Figure 6.11c as an example, the players have the following assignments. The middle front (MF) and right front (RF) players block the ball. Since the left front (LF) player is nôt blocking, he or she drops back to (not behind) the 3-meter line to dig sharp-angle spikes and soft spikes dinked inside (left of) the block. The left back (LB) player digs cross-court spikes passing inside (left of) the block. The middle back (MB) player takes balls hit deep along the baseline. The right back (RB) player digs spikes hit down the line and soft spikes just over the block. Specifics of player position responsibilities for the 4-deep defense are listed in Table 6.1.

TABLE 6.1
PLAYER POSITION RESPONSIBILITIES FOR THE 4-DEEP DEFENSE*

POSITION	RESPONSIBILITIES
Middle Front and Right Front (MF and RF)	Block.
Right Back (RB)	Spikes hit down the line. Dinks over block.
Middle Back (MB)	Deep spikes over the block. Cover entire baseline for spike deflections off block.
Left Back (LB)	Hard cross-court spikes.
Left Front (LF)	Sharp-angle spikes. Dinks passing inside of block.

*Refer to Figure 6.11c.

Suggested learning experience. The demonstrations and lead-up game experiences recommended for learning the 4-deep defense are identical to those outlined for the 3-deep defense. The reader is referred to chapter 5 (refer to Figure 6.11 rather than 5.22).

Defense-Offense Transition

The notion of dynamic team transition from offense to defense (or vice versa) was discussed at length in chapter 5 with regard to the 3-deep defense. The reader is referred to chapter 5 for a review of these basic concepts.

Execution. The transitional situations that arise during the execution of a rally are illustrated in Figure 6.12.

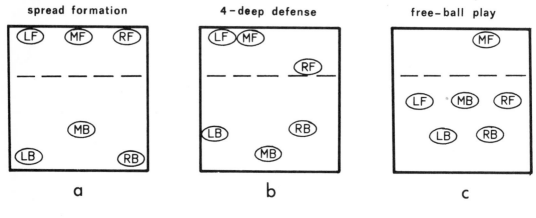

spread formation   4-deep defense   free-ball play

a   b   c

FIGURE 6.12

The defensive spread formation for the 4-deep defense is depicted in Figure 6.12a. A team assumes this formation when they serve and immediately after spiking a ball across the net (transition from c to a). When a team is in the defensive spread formation, one of two things generally occurs. First, the team may be required to defend against a spike as in Figure 6.12b (transition from a to b); or second, the team may drop back into an offensive W-formation (transition from a to c). This event occurs when the opposing team does not spike the ball, but merely bumps or sets the ball across the net (free ball). Conversely, a team that starts on offense (W-receiving formation) must be prepared to go on defense as soon as they volley the ball back across the net (transition from c to a).

Suggested learning experiences. The demonstrations and lead-up game experiences recommended for teaching team transition concepts when using the 4-deep defense are identical to those outlined for the 3-deep defense. The reader is referred to the discussion of team transition in chapter 5.

The 4-2 Offense

In the beginning progression (chapter 5) the basic offense taught was a straight W-formation with the middle front player doing the setting (regardless of this person's capabilities). In the 4-2 offense, the concept of *switching* is used to get the best spikers spiking and the best setter setting. In the 4-2 offense, switching involves the changing of positions the instant the ball is served. The switch is done in a way that maintains the integrity of the W-formation and requires a minimum of player movement.

In general, the purpose of offensive switching is to place a good setter, who is in a spiker's position (left or right front), into the center front position for setting purposes. Additionally, a good spiker who is in the middle front rotational position switches into a spiking position. The 4-2 offense provides a systematic approach for executing these favorable outcomes in an organized and pre-determined manner.

Execution. Team members utilizing the 4-2 offense are assigned one of three specialized player positions. These positions are the setter (S), the on-hand or power hitter (P), and the off-hand or weak-side hitter (W). When a setter is on the front row, he or she acts as the setter on every play. When a power hitter (P) is on the front row, he or she receives and spikes from the on-hand position twice and the off-hand once. Conversely, weak-side hitters (W) hit twice from the off-hand position of the net and once from the on-hand side.

In setting up the 4-2 player alignment, the two best spikers are designated as power hitters (P). The actual W-receiving formation positions for the first three rotations are illustrated in Figure 6.13 (the last three rotations are identical to the first three but with different members). The players are identified in Figure 6.13 as being power hitters (P), weak-side hitters (W), and setters (S). Players are further identified according to their serving order (e.g., player P_1 is the first server). The top row of the figure shows basic rotational positions (a_1, b_1, and c_1), while the bottom row shows the corresponding W-formation positions (a_2, b_2, and c_2).

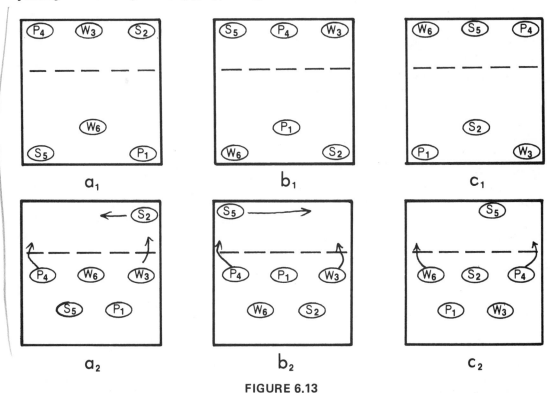

FIGURE 6.13

In Figure 6.13a_2, the middle front weak-side (W_3) spiker is shown switching positions with the right front setter (S_2). In this situation, just prior to the service, the middle back (W_6) player must be slightly behind the middle front (W_3) player, and the right front (S_2) must be to the right of the middle front (W_3) player. In Figure 6.13b_2, the middle front power hitter (P_4) is shown switching positions with the left front setter (S_5). In this situation, just prior to the service, the middle back (P_1) player must be slightly behind the middle front (P_4) player, and the left front (S_5) must be to the left of the middle front (P_4) player. Finally, in Figure 6.13c_2, no switching is necessary since the setter (S_5) is already in the setter's position. In all three situations (as diagrammed), the setter remains in the middle front position (once the switch is made) until the ball is dead.
position (once the switch is made) until the ball is dead.

Suggested learning experiences. The following demonstrations and lead-up game experiences will help the student understand the 4-2 offense.

1. Using group or team captains, review the W-receiving formation offense as taught in chapter 5 (middle front player sets). In each rotational position, point out the advantage or disadvantage of having the middle front player do all the setting. For example, in at least two positions, the best spikers (probably the worst setters) will be setting the ball, and in at least two positions, the best setters (probably the worst spikers) will be in the on-hand spiking positions.

2. Again, using group or team captains, demonstrate the 4-2 offense to the class. Go through the entire six-person rotation, showing how team members utilize the W-formation for reception and execute the switch when the ball is served. Point out the possible overlap situations. Explain clearly how the players can be so far from their rotational positions and yet not be out of position. Make sure each player is identified clearly in terms of specialized positions. For example, setters could be clearly identified by red shirts. Discuss receiving and spiking responsibilities and answer questions (see Figure 6.13).

3. The above court demonstration is repeated on each individual court with the group and team members being the participants and the group leaders (captains) doing the directing. The captain leads the team through at least two complete six-position rotations. After each six-position rotation, the team members change roles (setters become power hitters, weak-side hitters become setters, etc.)

4. Students next practice the 4-2 offense in a lead-up game situation. Players take their positions on the court. The team (Team A) practicing the 4-2 offense assumes the W-receiving formation. The opposing team (Team B) assumes the spread formation for the 4-deep defense. The team serving the ball (Team B) will serve five balls in succession. After each serve, the ball is played until it is dead. (Note: *Once the setter switches to the setter's position, he or she stays there until the ball is dead. In this way, the free-ball play and team transition from offense to defense are unchanged.*) Regardless of which side wins a "point," Team B continues to serve. After the five serves, both teams rotate one position. The same team that served before (Team B), serves another five times. This continues until Team B has served 30 balls. After 30 serves by one team, the two teams change roles and Team A serves 30 balls.

5. Teams practice the 4-2 offense in a game situation. Instructor and/or team captains should stop play to make corrective adjustments in the offense when necessary.

Spike Coverage

Spike coverage is the act of backing up your own team's spiker in case the spike is blocked. Spike coverage is to volleyball as rebounding is to basketball. It is a concept that can be learned by the intermediate performer and must be mastered by the advanced performer. Among competitive teams, effective spike coverage often separates the winners from the losers. Spike coverage assignments depend to a certain degree upon the type of offense used. In this chapter, it will be described in reference to the 4-2 offense.

Execution. Figure 6.14 shows a team (a) in W-receiving formation for serve, (b) executing spike coverage for an on-hand spike, and (c) executing spike coverage for an off-hand spike. For simplicity, the players have been identified in terms of their court positions. In addition, the hitter (H) and setter (S) have been identified with subscripts. The blockers (X) are also indicated. In both coverage situations (on-hand and off-hand), it is clear that spike coverage entails two semicircular lines of defense. One surrounds the hitter from in front of the 3-meter (10-ft) line, while the other is in the backcourt. The former is composed of three players and the latter of only two. The setter (MF_s) and the middle back (MB) players are involved in close spike coverage whether the ball is set to the on- or to the off-hand spikers. The third person to be involved in short spike coverage is always the player immediately behind the hitter. The two deep-coverage players position themselves in the seams between the short-coverage players.

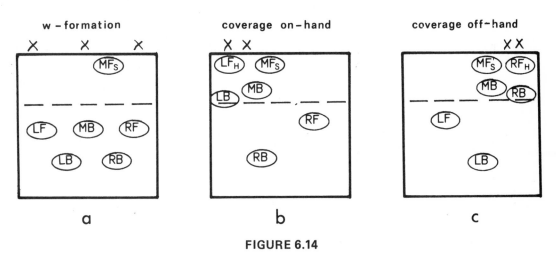

FIGURE 6.14

In anticipation of the ball coming to them, the short-coverage players surround the spiker as illustrated in Photo 6.5.

Suggested learning experiences. The basic steps followed for teaching the 4-2 offense are repeated, with the inclusion of spike coverage (see 4-2 offense in this chapter).

SUGGESTED STUDENT PROJECTS

1. Select one of the skills covered in this chapter and practice teaching it to a classmate.

2. Go to a volleyball match and analyze play in terms of individual skill performance. Write down errors that you can observe on skills covered in this chapter.

3. While at a volleyball match, identify the type of defense the teams are using. Write down errors in execution.

PHOTO 6.5
Spike coverage positions of players surrounding the spiker.

4. Prepare a bulletin-board display in which you compare the defense covered in this chapter with the 3-deep defense covered in chapter 5.

5. Diagram the 4-2 offense through six complete rotations.

6. Compose a 20-question true-false test over the rules listed in Box 5.1 and the clarifications given in micro-unit 3 of the sample teaching progression in chapter 6. In addition, compose a 20-question multiple-choice test on the skill and team strategies sections of chapter 6.

REFERENCES

NFSHSA. *National Federation Edition Volleyball Rules (1978-79).* Elgin, Illinois: National Federation of State High School Associations, 1978.
USVBA. *United States Volleyball Association Official Guide (1979).* San Francisco: United States Volleyball Association Publications, 1978.

7

Volleyball Instruction for Advanced Performers

This chapter on teaching volleyball to advanced-level students is also patterned after the organizational format of chapter 5. Section one will be composed of a sample teaching progression of 30 or 20 micro-units; section two will elaborate on the techniques of teaching the fundamental skills introduced in the progression; and section three will discuss the execution and teaching of team strategies of play.

Skills and strategies taught to beginners and intermediate performers will need to be reviewed for the students in the advanced class. Before teaching a unit on volleyball to advanced performers, the instructor should be thoroughly familiar with the material discussed in chapters 5 and 6. Most of the skills and team strategies outlined in the progression will be discussed in this chapter.

SAMPLE TEACHING PROGRESSION

As in chapters 5 and 6, this progression for intermediate students is composed of 30 micro-units of instruction. By eliminating the micro-units that are marked with an asterisk (*), the progression may be shortened to 20 micro-units (days).

Micro-Unit 1. Class organization
    a. Introductions.
    b. Attendance and grading procedures.
    c. Required wearing apparel, shower and locker room procedures.
    d. Instruction on set-up and take-down of nets.
    e. Explain roll call procedures.

*Micro-Unit 2. Testing and organization
    a. Pre-testing on the following skill tests:
        1. Brumbach forearm passing wall-volley test.
        2. AAHPER face passing wall-volley test.
    b. Use skill test scores to organize class into homogeneous team groupings.

Micro-Unit 3. Review rules and play volleyball
    a. Introduce and briefly discuss the rules outlines in Box 7.1. (The advanced performer who participates in organized competition will need to understand these rules.)
    b. Play volleyball for the purpose of observing general knowledge and skill level of students.

BOX 7.1
ADDITIONAL RULES FOR THE ADVANCED PLAYER

USVBA*	NFSHSA
1. Net antennas are attached vertically to and on the outside edge of the tape markers (sidelines).	1. Net antennas are attached to the net 8.5 inches outside the vertical tape markers (sidelines).
2. The court shall be 18 meters (59 ft) long and 9 meters (29.5 ft) wide.	2. The court shall be 60 feet long and 30 wide.
3. If a team has fewer than six players after the start of a match, play shall *not* continue.	3. If a team has fewer than six players after the start of a match, play *shall* continue.
4. A player may enter a game one time (excluding starting the game). A team is allowed six substitutions per game.	4. A player is limited to three entries during a game (including starting the game). A team is allowed an unlimited number of team substitutions.
5. Only one hand may be used to strike the ball for serve. The ball must be tossed to be hit.	5. During service, the ball may be hit with one or both hands. The ball does not have to be tossed to be hit.
6. A team is allowed two 30-second time-outs per game.	6. A team is allowed two 60-second time-outs per game. In addition, when time has expired or the score is tied at 14-14, one additional time-out is allowed each team.
7. Requesting a third time-out will be refused (no penalty).	7. Requesting a third time-out results in a penalty of point or side-out.
8. Simultaneous hitting of the ball by members of same team (not in act of blocking) counts as two hits and neither of the two players may make the next play on the ball.	8. Simultaneous contacts by members of same team is permitted and counts as one hit.
9. The server is given 5 seconds to release the ball for the serve (additional 5 seconds allowed if the ball allowed to drop to floor).	9. Service must be made within 5 seconds of referee's whistle.
10. A backline player may be involved in a block attempt at the net, but if *any* member of that block touches the ball it is a foul.	10. A backline player may not be involved in a block attempt at the net.
11. A frontline player may block a served ball before it crosses the net.	11. A frontline player may *not* block a served ball before it crosses the net.

*USBA and NAGWS (AIAW) rules are identical in most respects. In terms of substitutions, however, the NAGWS rules allow a player to enter the game three times (including starting the game) and in addition allow 12 team substitutions.

Micro-Unit 4. Teach the overhand Japanese floating serve (roundhouse)

 a. Discussion.

 b. Demonstration.

 c. Drills for practice.

 d. Utilize Japanese floating serve in game situation.

*Micro-Unit 5. Japanese floating serve, continued

 a. Discussion.

 b. Drills for practice.

 c. Utilize in game situation.

Micro-Unit 6. Teach the soft spike or "dink"

 a. Discussion

 b. Demonstration.

 c. Drills for practice.

 d. Utilize the dink in a game situation.

Micro-Unit 7. Teach the forward drive

 a. Discussion.

 b. Demonstration.

 c. Drills for practice.

 d. Utilize the dive in a game situation.

*Micro-Unit 8. The forward dive, continued

 a. Discussion.

 b. Drills for practice.

 c. Utilize the dive in game situation.

Micro-Unit 9. Teach advanced defensive blocking technique

 a. One-on-one blocking.

 b. Lateral step techniques.

 c. Watching the attacker.

 d. Utilize techniques in game situation.

Micro-Unit 10. Introduce the 3-attack offense

 a. Discussion.

 b. Demonstration.

 c. Learning experiences for practice.

Micro-Unit 11. Teach advanced setting techniques for 3-attack offense

 a. Discussion.

 b. Demonstration.

 c. Drills for practice.

*Micro-Unit 12. Advanced setting techniques, continued

 a. Discussion.

 b. Demonstration.

 c. Practice in game situation.

Micro-Unit 13. Review the following defensive team concepts
    a. 3-deep defense.
    b. 4-deep defense.
    c. Free-ball transition.

Micro-Unit 14. The 3-attack offense and spike coverage
    a. Discussion.
    b. Demonstration.
    c. Learning experiences for practice.
    d. Practice spike coverage in game situation.

Micro-Unit 15. Transition from offense (3-attack offense) to defense
    a. Discussion.
    b. Demonstration.
    c. Learning experiences for practice.
    d. Practice transition in game situation.

Micro-Unit 16. Introduce defensive switching concepts
    a. Discussion.
    b. Demonstration.
    c. Learning experiences for practice.
    d. Utilize defensive switching in game situation.

*Micro-Unit 17. Testing and review
    a. Administer short true-false test on rules in Box 7.1.
    b. Review skills and team tactics taught.

*Micro-Unit 18. Play volleyball
    a. Instructor serves as a referee for 10 minutes on each court.
    b. Instructor looks for areas of skill and team strategy weaknesses.

*Micro-Unit 19. Review and provide mini-units of instruction on weak areas identified in Micro-Unit 18

*Micro-Unit 20. Intra-class volleyball tournament

*Micro-Unit 21. Intra-class volleyball tournament

*Micro-Unit 22. Intra-class volleyball tournament

Micro-Unit 23. Intra-class volleyball tournament

Micro-Unit 24. Intra-class volleyball tournament

Micro-Unit 25. Intra-class volleyball tournament

Micro-Unit 26. Intra-class volleyball tournament

Micro-Unit 27. Intra-class volleyball tournament

Micro-Unit 28. Volleyball skill testing (See chapter 8)

Micro-Unit 29. Physical fitness testing (See chapter 8)

Micro-Unit 30. Written examination on skill and team strategy techniques
   discussed during unit of instruction.

TEACHING THE FUNDAMENTAL SKILLS

Each of the fundamental skills covered in this section will be discussed in terms of execution and drills for practice. The teacher is reminded that appropriate drills may be selected from those provided.

The Japanese Floating Serve

The Japanese floater is a roundhouse serve in which the ball is contacted directly above the head. Like the overhand floater, the Japanese floating serve is difficult to receive because it has an unpredictable flight pattern. Few American volleyball players learn the Japanese roundhouse serve because it means a temporary loss of serving effectiveness while they learn it. When mastered, however, the serve may be hit with great force and follows a dropping side-to-side flight pattern (Scates, 1976).

Execution. The execution of the Japanese floater serve is illustrated in Photo Sequence 7.1. As observed in the photo sequence the server starts with the body sideways to the net. The ball is tossed without spin about 1 meter (about 3 ft) above the head. As the server steps forward with the lead leg, the striking arm is extended backward into hitting position (arm points away from net). The ball is contacted at full extension of the arm directly over the head. The ball is contacted in the center of its axis by the heel of the striking hand (hand is open). The ball is hit firmly, but with little follow-through. The entire serving action is accomplished with shoulder rotation and without elbow flexion (bending the elbow).

PHOTO SEQUENCE 7.1
Execution of the Japanese roundhouse floating serve.

The basic arm-movement patterns involved in the Japanese roundhouse serve are not similar to the throwing action involved in the overhand floater taught in chapter 6. For this reason, volleyball players who have never mastered the throwing action involved in the traditional overhand serve often learn the roundhouse serve with ease.

Drills for practice. The suggested drills for learning the Japanese floating serve are identical to those given for the underhand floating serve in chapter 5.

The Soft Spike (Dink)

The dink spike is to volleyball as the change-up slow curve is to baseball. If a baseball pitcher had only one pitch, a fast ball, it would not be long before the hitters would be timing their swings for base hits. However, the experienced pitcher keeps the batter from "sitting" on the fast ball by throwing a few slow curves. This keeps the batter "honest" and forces him or her to adjust to each pitch separately. In volleyball, the advanced volleyball spiker must learn to keep the defense "honest" by hitting a few change-ups (dink spikes). This keeps the defense from playing deep for hard spikes only, since they must also worry about a soft spike that would fall in front of them.

Execution. In describing the soft spike, the reader is first referred to the spiking section of chapter 5. The execution of the soft spike is identical to the execution of the basic power spike right up to, but not including, ball contact. In fact, for the dink to be successful, the defense must believe that a regular power spike is forthcoming.

The three pictures in Photo Sequence 7.2 illustrate the soft spike. As can be observed, the ball is contacted at the top of the spiker's jump and with the hitting arm fully extended. Actual ball contact

PHOTO SEQUENCE 7.2
Execution of the soft spike against a tandem block. Pictures reproduced with permission from K. Herzog, *Volleyball Movements in Photographic Sequence* (Ottawa, Ontario: Canadian Volleyball Association, 1976).

takes place directly above the spiker's head and with the fingers of the spiking hand. Upon contact, the hand is slightly extended at the wrist. As follow-through is made, the fingers and wrist joint are flexed. The hand and finger control involved in the dink shot is similar to that involved in setting. As with the set, if the ball comes noticeably to rest or is directed, the referee will rule an illegal play.

In the soft spike, the ball should be dinked just barely over the blocker's hands and not too deep. Dinking the ball low into the blocker's hands will result in a "stuff," while dinking the ball too high or too deep will allow the backcourt defensive players time to get under the ball. Ideal placement of the dink shot will often depend on the expectations and type of defense used by the defensive team.

Drills for practice. The soft spike is much more difficult to learn than might be expected. Many otherwise good volleyball players fail to practice the dink shot and for this reason are rarely successful with it. The following drills used in conjunction with the spiking drills given in chapters 5 and 6 (pages 36-38 and pages 57-58) will help make a complete spiker out of the advanced performer.

1. Soft spike into wall. This drill is similar to the wall-spiking drill depicted in Figure 5.12 of chapter 5. However, instead of hitting the ball into the ground, the ball is dinked into the wall. The learner starts about 2 meters (about 7 ft) from the wall and begins each practice spike by tossing the ball to himself or herself (as in the overhand serve). Students are spaced 3 meters (about 10 ft) apart.

2. Practicing the dink with partner. (See Figure 7.1.) This drill is like a setting drill in which two players set the ball back and forth. In this case, however, one partner sets the ball while the other practices dinking the ball back. The players start about 3 meters (about 10 ft) apart. The setter sets the ball about 3 meters into the air, while the spiker dinks the ball without an arc back to the setter. Pairs of students are spaced equally around gym area.

3. Practicing the soft spike with net. This drill is exactly like several drills described in chapters 5 and 6 (see drill depicted in Figure 5.13) in which the learner practices spiking. In this drill, the learner practices the soft spike in conjunction with the power spike. The object is to make each spike look exactly alike up to the point of ball contact. Using two spiking lines, twelve students can practice on a single net.

4. Practicing the soft spike with a block. (See Figure 7.2.) This drill is also very similar to several drills described in chapters 5 and 6 (see Figure 5.20) in which the learner practices spiking. The

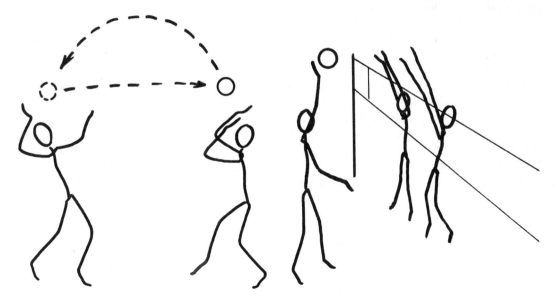

FIGURE 7.1   FIGURE 7.2

learner practices dinking the ball just over the block into target areas behind the block. It is also helpful if actual backcourt defenders are involved since they will provide immediate feedback on the effectiveness of each soft spike attempt. Using two spiking lines, twelve students can practice on a single net.

The Forward Dive

The forward dive, like the Japanese roll (see chapter 6), is a defensive technique designed to increase a player's range of effectiveness. When first introduced in the United States (1964-65), it was considered very much a desperation-type skill. While many coaches and teachers advocated its use, few players took it seriously. Today, however, it is taken seriously by almost every serious-minded player and coach. For many volleyball players, the forward dive has replaced the Japanese roll as the primary means for going after balls that require body contact with the floor. In fact, the term "forward" is really somewhat misleading, since it implies that only balls in front of a person are played. In a sense this is true, but only after an initial adjustment to direct the front of the body towards the ball. For example, a dive can be used to get a ball that initially is destined to land behind and to the side of a defensive player.

Execution. In execution of the forward dive, six basic components can be identified. They are described below and illustrated in Photo Sequence 7.3.

1. The athlete must initially move in the direction of the ball or point of intersection with the ball. Sometimes this only involves one step and a short distance, but in some cases it involves a number of yards and considerable speed development.

2. Concurrently with initiating movement in the direction of the ball, the learner must noticeably lower the center of gravity just prior to leaving the ground. This is done by bending forward at the hip joint and by flexing the knee joints.

3. With the center of gravity low and the body moving in the direction of the ball, the next step is to propel the body horizontally into the air by extending and vaulting off the lead leg. It is important to emphasize, here, that the body is propelled horizontally into the air and not at an angle greater than zero degrees above the horizontal plane (head higher than feet).

4. At some point after leaving the ground and before the hands touch the floor, the individual must hit the volleyball. While this aspect of the forward dive is critical to the goal aspect of the dive, it is very difficult to perfect until the skill aspects of the dive itself have been mastered. Actual contact with the ball should occur on the forearms of both extended arms if possible (forearm pass). Usually, however, only the easier balls can be played in this manner. Other methods of contacting the ball are with a closed fist, on the heel of the open hand, and, in many instances, with the back of the closed or open hand. The actual ball contact aspect of the forward dive must be practiced as much as the dive itself. It is also desirable that the athlete gain the ability to contact the ball with either hand, depending on which side of the body the ball is on.

5. In completing the dive, the athlete must make a successful landing. In accomplishing this, initial contact with the floor is made with the hands spread wide and out in front of the body. At this point, the athlete's body should be in a swan-dive position. The back is arched, the knees are flexed, the hip joint is hyperextended, and the head is up and extended backwards.

6. Once contact has been made with the floor by the hands, the momentum of the dive is transferred to the lower chest and abdominal region of the body. The blow to the chest and stomach is dissipated by allowing the body to slide forward on the gym floor. This particular action is relatively

PHOTO SEQUENCE 7.3
Execution of the forward dive.

easy when the athletes are sweaty and are playing on a hardwood floor. However, sliding on the floor becomes a little more difficult when playing on artificial turf. While most artificial turf floors retard the sliding action considerably, it is not altogether eliminated. The real danger that occurs and must be watched for is the use of rubberized materials (lettering) on the front of jerseys. From a safety standpoint, it is strongly recommended that rubberized numbers and insignias not be placed on the uniforms. A teaching technique that may be utilized to help students make proper body contact with the floor is shown in Photo Sequence 7.4.

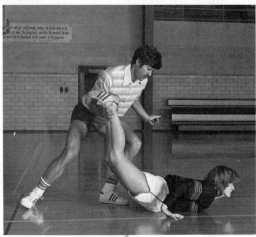

PHOTO SEQUENCE 7.4
Wheelbarrow learning progression for the forward dive.

Drills for practice. The following drills (in sequence) are suggested for use in developing skill in the forward dive.

1. Group practice without a ball. In this drill, the instructor leads the entire class through a step-by-step progression of the forward dive (see Box 7.2). The group drill should continue until all students can execute the dive with confidence. See Figure 6.9 and the drill associated with it for further instructions.

BOX 7.2
LEARNING PROGRESSION FOR THE DIVE

Step 1. Have students fall forward, breaking their fall with their hands. If they can do this, they have sufficient strength to execute the dive.

Step 2. Have students lower their center of gravity by flexing knees and bending at hips, and then extending and falling forward as before. Explain that the center of gravity is also lowered in executing the dive.

Step 3. Utilizing the wheelbarrow concept as depicted in Photo Sequence 7.4, have the students practice the "swan" dive.

Step 4. Without assistance from another student, have each student execute the "swan" dive by himself or herself.

Step 5. With the assistance of a three- to four-step approach, have students practice completing the dive by sliding forward on their chest and abdominal area.

Step 6. Remind the students of the following key elements in executing the dive:
    a. Keep chin up!
    b. Arch the back.
    c. Do not allow knees or feet to touch the floor until after completion of dive.

2. Small-group instruction without ball. The students break up into small groups of approximately six per group. The students practice the forward dive with assistance from a skilled group member (assign a skilled student to each group, if possible). The instructor rotates between groups and provides assistance where needed. Students should gain confidence in the basic dive without a ball before trying the next drill. Many students may benefit from practice on a wrestling or tumbling mat if one is available.

3. Ball roll and dive drill. (See Figure 7.3.) Two students face each other with a distance of 8 meters (about 26 ft) separating them. One of the two students rolls the ball (without a bounce) to the other. His or her partner takes several lead steps in the direction of the ball, lowers the center

FIGURE 7.3

of gravity, reaches down and scoops the ball up with the fingers of one or both hands, and executes a forward dive to culminate the action. Partners take turns rolling the ball to each other until each has received ten balls. The drill can be expanded to involve six or more people by the formation of two opposing lines. In this case, a player goes to the end of the opposing line after rolling the ball or executing a dive.

4. Organized small group diving drill with ball. (See Figure 7.4.) The diver dives for ten balls in a row. The diver (D) stands between two tossers (T) who alternately toss balls that require maximum effort to reach. The shaggers (S) chase loose balls and make sure that tossers always have a ball ready to be tossed. For motivational purposes, the following formulas may be built into the drill: (a) the athlete must make 10 successful diving saves; (b) failure to touch a thrown ball before it hits the floor counts as a negative hit (adds on to the required 10); and (c) balls touched but not deemed successful count as zero hits.

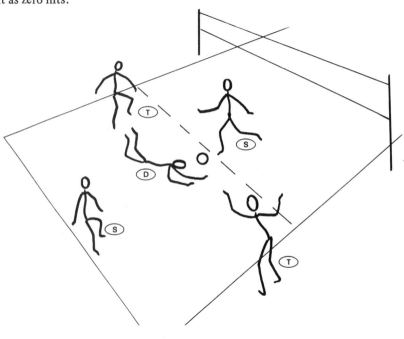

FIGURE 7.4

5. Pepper drill with ball. In this drill, two students stand 3 meters (about 10 ft) apart and hit the ball at each other (see Figure 6.10). The spiker hits the ball at the receiver in such a manner that the receiver must use the forward dive and other defensive techniques to field the ball. The drill can be expanded into a group drill by employing one hitter, two diggers, and several ball shaggers. Players take turns shagging, spiking, and diving. It is important to keep students spread out to avoid injuries caused from diving into each other.

Advanced Blocking Technique

Individual and tandem blocking technique was introduced in chapter 5. In this section we will expand the teaching and execution principles discussed in the chapter for beginners. As the advanced volleyball player encounters highly skilled offensive attacks, it is necessary that the student's defensive blocking skills become equally sophisticated. For clarity, each of the five concepts to be discussed will be covered separately.

1. One-on-one blocking. Up to this point, it has been assumed that tandem blocking was the rule. However, with the introduction of the 3-attack offense (to be discussed in this chapter), it is not always possible to effect a 2-person block.

a. Execution of one-on-one blocking. Figure 7.5 depicts each blocker at the net assuming a one-on-one blocking responsibility with the opposing spiker. It is his or her responsibiliy to determine the spiker's expected spiking angle and to move laterally to block it. It is the middle blocker's (MB) first responsibility to block the opposing middle spiker. However, the instant the middle blocker determines that the opposing spiker is not going to get the set, the middle blocker moves laterally to assist the line blockers in stopping their opponent (tandem block).

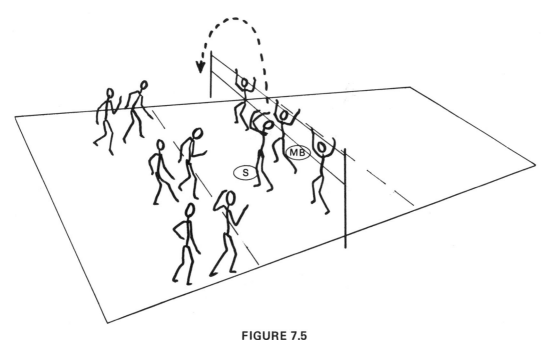

FIGURE 7.5

b. Drill for practice. The following drill will assist the teacher in teaching one-on-one blocking responsibility. (See Figure 7.5.) In this drill three blockers take positions opposing three spiking lines. The setter (S) sets the ball to each hitting line in turn. Each opposing blocker attempts to block the opposing spiker by himself or herself. Spikers rotate to different lines after spiking. Each blocker makes five blocking attempts at each blocking position before three new blockers rotate in. Play begins with the spiker whose turn it is to spike passing the ball to the setter.

2. Lateral movement of the middle blocker. If at all possible, the middle blocker must move laterally to form a tandem block with the line blocker when the ball is set outside. To be successful defensively, a team must be able to effect a tandem block at least 85 percent of the time.

a. Execution of lateral movement. There are three basic methods for moving laterally for blocking. These three methods are (a) the slide step, (b) the cross-over step, and (c) the jab cross-over step. The cross-over technique methods are the most common, since they allow the blocker full freedom for an arm swing as the body turns sideways from the net. The slide-step method, however, is the quickest (Cox, 1978). Regardless of which technique is used, it is important that it be practiced daily.

b. Drill for practice. With a few minor modifications, the drill as depicted in Figure 7.5 will assist the middle blocker in learning to respond laterally for blocking purposes. The modifications are (a) the pass from spiker to setter originates from the on-hand spiking line; (b) spiking lines are set randomly rather than in order; and (c) the middle blocker attempts to effect a tandem block whenever possible (85 percent of the time).

3. Turning the spike in. Unless line blockers are highly accomplished at turning the spike into the center of the opponents' court, a spiker who continually hits down-the-line can do much damage. If the down-the-line spike is not turned in, a large percentage of these balls will deflect off the block and go out of bounds on the spiker's side of the net. This, of course, results in a point or a side-out for the spiker's team, since there is nothing the defense can do to get at the ball.

a. Execution of turning the spike in. This particular technique is executed by the line blocker. It is accomplished by turning the outside hand in towards the center of the opponents' court at the same time the block is effected.

b. Drill for practice. Again, with a few minor modifications, the drill as depicted in Figure 7.5 will assist the line blocker (LB) in learning to turn the spike in. The modifications are (a) middle blocker attempts to effect a tandem block; (b) on-hand and off-hand spikers hit the ball down-the-line; and (c) line blockers (LB) attempt to turn the ball in.

4. Watching the attacker. The spiker's intended hitting direction can often be determined by studying the spiker's approach, jump, and arm swing.

a. Extension of watching the attacker. The blocker must never take his or her eyes off the assigned opponent. The flight of the ball is a secondary matter and should be watched peripherally by the blocker. This is especially true when the offense is using a sophisticated 3-attack offense. In practice, then, the blocker literally mirrors the movements of the opposing spiker.

b. Drill for practice (blind blocking drill). (See Figure 7.6.) This drill is designed to force the blocker(s) to watch the attacker and not the ball. The ball is lofted into spiking position by the

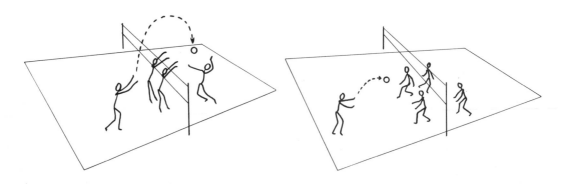

FIGURE 7.6   **FIGURE 7.7**

instructor from behind the block. The blockers never see the ball until it is hit. After the blockers have each had five block attempts from the middle and line positions, it is time to rotate.

5. Block recovery. There is a very high probability that if the ball is not blocked, it will be dug by a back-row player. If this happens, the ball may be heading right for the backsides of the blockers.

a. Execution of block recovery. The instant the spiked ball passes the block, the blockers should be anticipating that they may have to make the second play on the ball. They do this by spinning away from the net toward the backcourt. The direction of the turn should always be toward the center of the court and not to the sideline (e.g., right line blocker would turn counterclockwise along with middle blocker).

b. Drill for practice (block recovery drill). (See Figure 7.7.) Blockers practice spinning away from the net the instant the ball passes the block (after feet touch the floor). To assure that they are ready to play the ball, the instructor or skilled student lobs, tosses, and spikes balls at them as they turn. The blockers make the best play that they can on the ball. If possible, they would set the ball up for another front-line player to spike.

Advanced Setting Technique

Basic front and back setting techniques were introduced in chapters 5 and 6. This chapter will introduce four advanced setting techniques that are reserved for the skilled performer. For clarity, each of the four concepts will be introduced and discussed separately.

1. The jump set. Jump setting is a setting technique that can provide the skilled setter with added deception and maneuverability. It is not recommended for the beginner or the intermediate performer. In fact, the advanced performer should only use it when it serves a specific purpose. Jump setting just to be jumping is not good setting strategy. However, when the setter happens to be a front-row player, or the ball is set close to the net, the jump set can be highly effective. Both of these situations will force the opponents' middle blocker to commit himself or herself to a block attempt. This, in turn, cuts down the probability of the opposition forming an effective tandem block.

a. Execution of the jump set. As illustrated in Photo Sequence 7.5, the jump set, with the exception of the jump, is similar to the basic volley set discussed in chapter 5. As can be observed in Photo Sequence 7.5, the setter uses a two-footed take-off and a vigorous thrust of the arms to assist the take-off. Once in the air, the setter volleys the ball while at the peak of the jump. The ball itself must be above the setter's head and hands.

b. Drills for practice. The following drills will assist the teacher in teaching the jump set.

(1) Jump-setting line-passing drill. (See Figure 7.8.) This simple group drill is exactly like the passing line drill introduced in chapter 5 (Figure 5.9), with the exception that the setters jump set the ball. As before, the setter, after passing the ball across the net, moves to the right and goes to the end of the opposing line.

(2) Jump setting in pairs. (See Figure 7.9.) This is a highly skilled drill in which two students jump set the ball back and forth. It is done in such a manner that the ball remains almost stationary in the air. The players stand within one meter of each other. Not only is this drill good for setting technique, but it is very good for leg conditioning and timing.

2. The side set. As with the jump set, side setting can be an important technique to master. It should not be used by the beginner nor by the advanced performer when straight front and back setting are possible (it can become a habit). The technique is especially useful for setting balls that are extremely close to the net.

PHOTO SEQUENCE 7.5
Execution of the jump set.

FIGURE 7.8   **FIGURE 7.9**

a. Execution of the side set. As illustrated in Photo Sequence 7.6, side setting is executed from a position facing the net. If a player was to attempt a regular front or back set on a ball that was within 30 centimeters (about 12 in.) of the net, a net violation would certainly occur. Therefore, the setter positions himself or herself directly under the ball as indicated in the photo sequence. The setter's knees are bent, and the forearms are parallel to the net. In setting the ball, the setter's hands move up and sideways rather than forward or back. As long as the ball does not come to rest (noticeably) or is contacted twice, the play is legal.

b. Drills for practice.

(1) Side setting drill to partner. This drill is identical to the situation described in drill 2 for back setting in chapter 6, except that the ball is side set instead of back set. Specifically, two persons work in pairs. When the ball comes to a student, he or she first sets the ball to himself or herself and then rotates the body 90 degrees left or right and side sets it back to his or her partner. This continues, with both partners practicing front sets, back sets, and side sets. Students are distributed evenly around the gym for this drill.

(2) Side setting to partner while facing wall. (See Figure 7.10.) Two students practice side setting the ball back and forth to each other while facing a flat wall. In executing the drill, students must be within one meter (about 3 ft) of the flat wall and have forearms parallel with the wall. After 30 or 40 trials, the students change positions so that each gains practice at side setting left and right. Students (pairs) should be 3 meters (about 10 ft) apart. Approximately five pairs of students could work along a 25-meter (about 82-ft) wall.

(3) Side setting to partner while facing net. This drill is exactly like the drill depicted in Figure 7.10, except a net is used instead of a wall. The advantage of the net over the wall is that the net is more realistic. However, given a shortage of available nets, the use of flat walls is helpful. Again, students change positions after 30 to 40 side sets, so that both performers get practice side setting left and right. Generally, two pairs of students can practice on each side of a single net.

3. The screw-under technique. In chapter 6 the Japanese roll was primarily discussed in conjunction with a one-hand dig. When the Japanese roll (or parts of it) is used in setting, the technique is

PHOTO SEQUENCE 7.6
Execution of the side set when the ball is close to the net.

referred to as the screw-under technique (Scates, 1976). The advanced volleyball player should make it a rule to use the face pass for setting, rather than the forearm pass, on every possible play. In order to accomplish this goal, it is often necessary to use the Japanese roll to get under the ball.

a. Execution of the screw-under technique for setting. As illustrated in Photo Sequence 7.7, the screw-under technique for setting is identical to the Japanese roll for a one-arm dig, except for the manner in which the ball is played (compare with Photo Sequence 6.4). The setter first moves laterally to get near the ball. Next, the setter collapses the lead leg and literally "screws" the body underneath the ball. From this position, the ball is set, and follow-through is accomplished with the Japanese roll.

b. Drills for practice. The foundation of the screw-under technique is the ability to execute a Japanese roll (without ball) and to set the ball forward, back, or sideward. If these techniques are not mastered, the student should be instructed to practice the various drills in chapters 5 and 6 designed to accomplish this. The following two drills are suggested.

PHOTO SEQUENCE 7.7
Execution of the screw-under technique for setting.

(1) Screw-under technique drill for two students. (See Figure 7.11.) This drill is identical to the situation described in drill 3 for the Japanese roll in chapter 6, except the ball is set, rather than dug, with one hand. The tosser should toss the ball 1.6 meters (about 5 ft) high and far enough away from the setter so that a long lead step is required to get ten balls and set the same. As in the earlier drill, no deception in tossing direction should be allowed. Students work in pairs and are distributed evenly around the gym.

(2) Setting bad passes to spikers. (See Figure 7.12.) The setter utilizes the screw-under technique to get under and set the ball to real spikers. Either two or three spiking lines may be used. In Figure 7.12 only two lines are used. In either case, the instructor or an informed student lobs difficult-to-set balls to the setter. In each case, the setter makes a maximum effort to set the ball with the fingers. If the setter does not have to use the screw-under technique on at least 50 percent of the tosses, the lobs are too easy.

4. Advanced play sets. The basic sets in the game of volleyball are relatively high sets to the on-hand and off-hand corners of the net, and, with the introduction of the 3-attack offense, a high set to center position of the net. In fact, the three basic sets described above and illustrated in Figure 7.13 are all that are really needed to have a successful volleyball team. This is especially true if your spikers are tall, jump well, and hit with consistency. Nevertheless, numerous types of "quick"

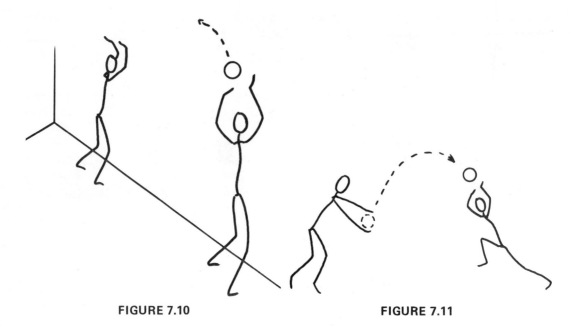

FIGURE 7.10   **FIGURE 7.11**

sets have become extremely popular with American teams. This is primarily due to the flashy influence of the Japanese and oriental style of play. When a team employs various "quick" sets in an organized system of play, it is referred to as a *multiple attack*.

    a. Execution of the advanced play sets. In this section, four basic play sets will be discussed. As illustrated in Figure 7.14, they are the "one set," the "front two set," the "back two set," and the "three" or "shoot set."

    (1) The one set. The one set is the basic set for the multiple attack offense. Regardless of what the other spikers may be getting, the middle attacker looks for the one set. It is set about 30 to 60 centimeters (about 1 to 2 ft) above the net and the same distance in front of the setter. When the ball is properly hit, the spiker is in the air before the ball is set.

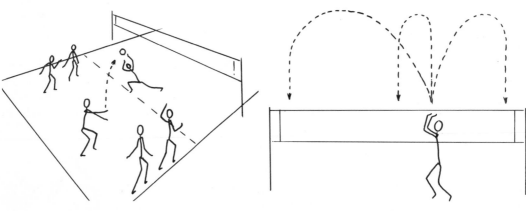

FIGURE 7.12   **FIGURE 7.13**

(2) The front two set. The front two set is generally hit by the on-hand spiker rather than the middle attacker. It is set about 1.5 meters (about 5 ft) above the net and the same distance in front of the setter.

(3) The back two set. The back two is set exactly like the front two except it is hit by the off-hand hitter rather than the on-hand hitter.

(4) The three, or shoot, set. The shoot set is a ball spiked exclusively by the on-hand hitter. It is set at a speed twice as fast as the normal set. Theoretically, this gives the spiker an advantage, since the tandem block will not have time to form. As indicated in Figure 7.14, the ball is set to the on-hand corner of the net and at its apex is about 1.5 meters (about 5 ft) above the net.

b. Drill for practice. Two basic classes of drills are suggested for practicing the multiple offense play sets. The first type, with the elimination of the blockers, is illustrated in Figure 7.5. The spikers merely indicate to the setter what kind of set they want. The second type, described next, is more specialized.

Specialized play set drill. (See Figure 7.15.) In this drill two lines are formed. One line is a tossing line, the other a spiking line. The exact placement of the lines depends upon the set being practiced. As indicated in Figure 7.15 for the back two set, the individual at the head of the tossing line lobs or face passes the ball to the setter. The setter, in turn, back sets the ball to the person at the head of the spiking line. Spikers chase their own spike and get into the tossing line. Tossers go to spiking lines.

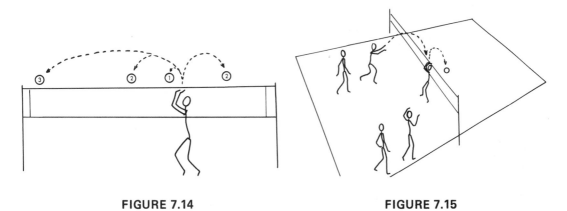

FIGURE 7.14   **FIGURE 7.15**

EXECUTION AND TEACHING TEAM STRATEGIES OF PLAY

In addition to a review of certain team concepts of play for beginners and intermediate students (W-receiving formation, 3- and 4-deep defense), the advanced class should be taught several new team strategies. These team strategies are (a) the 3-attack offense, (b) transition from defense to offense, (c) spike coverage, and (d) defensive switching. Each of these new team strategies will be discussed in terms of execution and suggested learning experiences.

The 3-Attack Offense

In the 4-2 offense (covered in chapter 6), one of the front-row players was designated as the setter. In the 3-attack offense, a back-row player is designated as the setter. This means, of course, that all three front-row players are eligible to spike the ball.

Execution. Team members utilizing the 3-attack offense are assigned one of three specialized player positions. These positions are middle blocker, setter, and technique. When a setter is on the back row, he or she acts as the setter on every play.

In setting up the 3-attack player alignment, the best two blockers (generally the best spikers, as well) are designated as middle blockers. The best setters are designated as setters. The technique player, while not the best blocker or setter, is often the best all-around player, since he or she must be able to do everything well.

The actual W-receiving formation positions for the first three rotations are illustrated in Figure 7.16. (The last three rotations are identical to the first three, but with different personnel.) The players are identified in Figure 7.16 as being middle blockers (MB), setters (S), or technique (T) players. They are further identified according to their serving order (e.g., player MB_1 is the first server). The top row of the figure shows basic rotational positions (a_1, b_1 and c_1). As illustrated in parts a_2, b_2, and c_2 of Figure 7.16, as soon as the ball is served, the setter penetrates to the right front position of the net. From this position (assuming an accurate pass), he or she sets one of the three eligible front-line attackers.

Suggested learning experiences. The following lead-up game experiences will help the student understand the 3-attack offense.

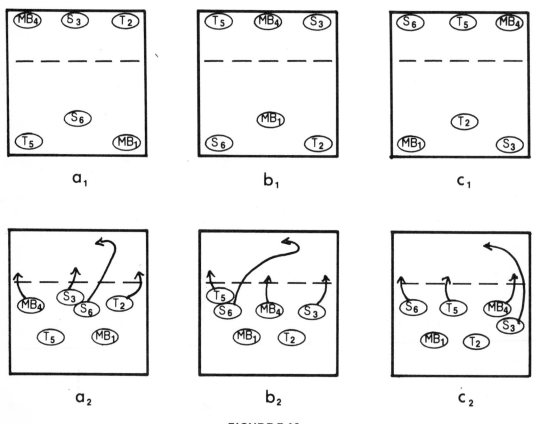

FIGURE 7.16

1. Using group or team captains, review and discuss the W-receiving formation as used in the 3-attack offense. From each rotational position, show how the setter penetrates forward to the setting position at the net. Make sure each player is identified clearly in terms of specialized positions (red shirts, etc.). Discuss any overlap problems that might occur and answer questions.

2. The above court demonstration is repeated on each individual court with the group and team members being the participants and the group leaders (captains) doing the directing. The captain leads the team through at least two six-person rotations. After each six-person rotation, the team members change roles (setters become middle blockers, middle blockers become technique players, etc.).

3. Students next practice the 3-attack offense in a lead-up game situation. Players take their positions on the court. The team practicing the 3-attack offense (Team A) assumes the W-receiving formation. The opposing team (Team B) assumes the spread formation for the 4-deep defense. The team serving the ball (Team B) will serve the ball five times in succession from each rotational position (the ball is dead as soon as the ball is spiked by the receiving team). After 30 serves by Team B the two teams change roles and Team A serves 30 balls.

4. Teams practice the 3-attack offense in a game situation. Instructor and/or team captains should stop play to make corrective adjustments in the offense when necessary.

Spike Coverage

Spike coverage is a concept that must be mastered by the advanced player. Specific spike coverage assignments depend to a certain degree upon the type of offense used. In this section, spike coverage is discussed with respect to the 3-attack offense.

Execution. Figure 7.17 shows a team (a) in W-formation for serve reception, (b) executing spike coverage for an on-hand spike, (c) executing spike coverage for a middle attack, and (d) executing spike coverage for an off-hand spike. For simplicity, the players have been identified in terms of their court positions. In addition, the hitter (H) and setter (S) have been identified with subscripts. The blockers (X) are also indicated. For the on-hand and off-hand situations (Figure 7.17b and d), spike coverage assignments are nearly identical to the 4-2 offense assignments (see Figure 6.14b and c). The one exception is that the middle front (MF) instead of the middle back (MB) player is involved in close spike coverage.

In the case of spike coverage for the middle attack, the reader is referred to Figure 7.17c. In this situation, short spike coverage (in front of 3-meter line) is effected by the setter and the other two spikers (left and right front players). Deep coverage is effected by the back-row players (in this case left back (LB) and right back (RB)

Suggested learning experiences. The basic steps for teaching the 3-attack offense are repeated, with the inclusion of spike coverage assignments.

Defense-Offense Transition

The concept of defense-offense transition (and vice versa) for both the 3-deep and the 4-deep defenses as they relate to the 2-attack offense was discussed in chapters 5 and 6. In this section we will discuss each defense as it relates to the 3-attack offense.

Execution. The execution of defense-to-offense transition will be explained first in terms of the 3-deep defense and second in terms of the 4-deep defense.

1. **Transition and the 3-deep defense.** In the 3-attack offense, the setter penetrates from a back-row position. Consequently, when the team makes the transition from offense to defense, the setter

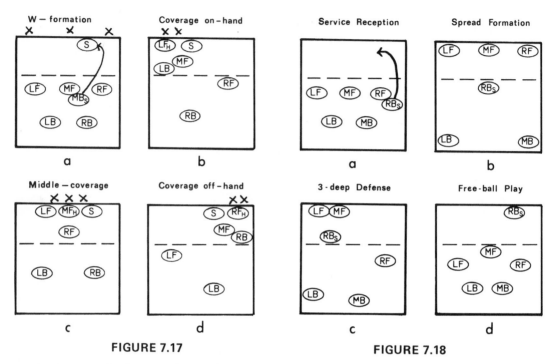

FIGURE 7.17　　　　　　　　　**FIGURE 7.18**

must return to a back-row position. The setter does not return to the position he or she came from (necessarily), but to a predetermined position. When a team is running a middle-up or 3-deep defense, the setter *always* becomes the middle-up player.

The transitional situations that occur during the course of rally are depicted in Figure 7.18. Beginning with service reception, Figure 7.18*a* shows the team in proper service rotation. As the ball is served, the setter (RB$_S$) penetrates forward to the setting position. The defensive spread formation for the 3-deep defense is depicted in Figure 7.18*b*. A team assumes this formation when they serve, and after spiking the ball across the net (transition from *a* to *b*). When a team is in the defensive spread formation, one of two things generally occurs. First, the team may be required to defend against a spike as in Figure 7.18*c* (transition from *b* to *c*); or second, the team may drop back into an offensive W-formation for a free ball (transition from *b* to *d*).

2. Transition and the 4-deep defense. When a team is running a 4-deep defense, the setter always becomes the right back defensive player (transition from offense to defense). The transitional situations that transpire during the course of a rally are depicted in Figure 7.19. Beginning with service reception, Figure 7.19*a* shows the team in proper service rotation. As the ball is served, the setter (MB$_S$) penetrates forward to the setting position. The defensive spread formation for the 4-deep defense is depicted in Figure 7.19*b*. When a team is in the defensive spread formation, one of two things generally occurs. First, the team may be required to defend against a spike as in Figure 7.19*c* (transition from *b* to *c*); or second, the team may drop back into an offensive W-formation for a free ball (transition from *b* to *d*).

Suggested learning experiences. The demonstrations and lead-up game experiences recommended for teaching team transition concepts (regardless of type of defense or offense) are outlined in the team transition section of chapter 5.

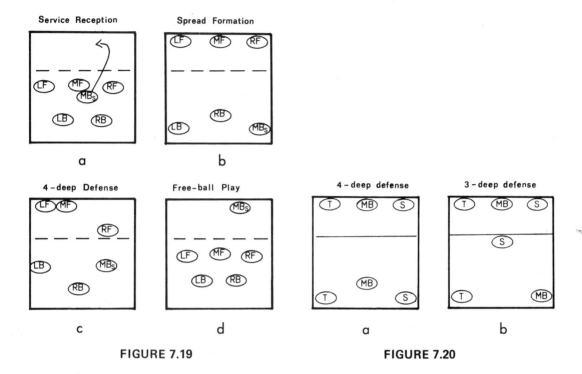

FIGURE 7.19   FIGURE 7.20

Defensive Switching

Offensive switching was introduced in chapter 6 in conjunction with the 4-2 offense. Specifically, upon service reception, the front-row setter would switch into the setter's position (see Figure 6.13), and a front row spiker would assume a hitter's position. This sort of switching was introduced to maximize the effectiveness of the offensive attack. For the same reason, switching positions for defensive reasons can be done to maximize the effectiveness of the defense.

Execution. For simplicity and clarity, the execution of defensive switching will be described first for the front row (blocking) and second for the back row (digging). Finally, a total team concept of defensive switching will be suggested.

1. Switching blockers. Blockers are switched to maximize the effectiveness of the block. Since the middle front player is potentially involved in every block situation, it makes sense that a team's best blocker should switch into this position. As the 3-attack offense has been set up, this person would be the middle blocker (MB). If defensive switching is employed, this specific switch should be effected whenever a team makes the transition from offense to defense (including when a team serves the ball).

2. Switching diggers. The basic back-row switch that is employed with the 3-attack offense is the one that switches the setter into a specific defensive alignment. Recall that with the 3-deep defense the setter switches into the middle-up position (Figure 7.18) and for the 4-deep defense the right back position (Figure 7.19). In addition to the setter switch, it is often desirable to switch a team's best digger into the left back (LB) digging position. The reason for this is that most spikes from the opposition are hit cross-court and from their on-hand position.

3. A team concept of defensive switching. When a team is serving the ball, certain predetermined switches are desirable. These basic switches are illustrated in Figure 7.20*a* for the 4-deep defense and Figure 7.20*b* for the 3-deep defense. These switches are effected the instant the ball is served, regardless of the service rotation positions of the players.

When a team makes the transition from offense to defense on a live ball, it is recommended that only the basic switches be effected (e.g., middle blocker to center front and setter switch in back row). With a great deal of practice, however, complete back-row switching can be accomplished efficiently.

Suggested learning experiences

1. Utilizing team captains or group leaders, illustrate the advantage to be gained by making defensive switches. Suggest ways that the switches can be accomplished most effectively.

2. Have the students practice defensive switching in a game situation. Suggest that they start with switching the middle blocker (MB) into the center front position on defense. When they have mastered this simple defensive switch, go into more advanced switches.

SUGGESTED STUDENT PROJECTS

1. Practice teaching either the Japanese forward dive or floating serve to a classmate.

2. In the 5-1 offense, a single player does all of the setting. See if you can diagram the 5-1 offense through six complete service reception rotational positions. (Hint: review chapter 9.)

3. Look at Figure 7.20 and explain why the various players are shown switching to the positions indicated.

4. Go to a high school volleyball match and keep track (paper and pencil) of the number and type of blocking errors that are made. What was the most common blocking error made? Suggest a cause and correction for each type of error observed. Refer to chapters 5 and 7 for suggestions.

5. Compose a 20-question true-false test from the rules listed in Box 7.1. In addition, compose a 20-question multiple-choice test on the skill and team strategies sections of chapter 7.

REFERENCES

Cox, R.H. "Choice Response Time Speeds of the Cross-over and Slide Steps as Used in Volleyball." *Research Quarterly,* 49 (1978), 430-436.

NFSHSA. *National Federation Edition Volleyball Rules (1978-79).* Elgin, Illinois: National Federation of State High School Associations, 1978.

Scates, A.E. *Winning Volleyball.* 2nd ed. Boston: Allyn and Bacon, Inc., 1976.

USVBA. *United States Volleyball Association Official Guide (1979).* San Francisco: United States Volleyball Association Publications, 1978.

Evaluation

At the beginning of a four- or six-week unit of instruction on volleyball, the teacher identifies specific terminal performance objectives that he or she expects the students to achieve. These objectives fall under the categories of physical fitness, skill acquisition, and cognitive, affective, and personal-social development. At the conclusion of the teaching unit, the teacher evaluates student performance to determine whether or not the student has achieved his or her objectives.

In two of the measurement categories (physical fitness and skill acquisition), performance norm tables have been included. However, the prospective or practicing teacher must resist the temptation to rely completely on these tables. Norm tables based on data gathered from the instructor's students will be much more valuable than a table developed by others. The procedures for developing norm tables based on percentiles are quite simple and are explained clearly in most measurement textbooks (see Johnson and Nelson, pp. 20-29).

SELECTED PERFORMANCE TESTS

This section is about specific tests that are recommended for evaluating performance in the various domains.

The Physical Fitness Domain

Because volleyball is a highly anaerobic activity, the selected fitness tests measure various skill-related rather than health-related aspects of physical fitness. To save time, the tests should be administered at several test stations with the assistance of student leaders.

1. **Vertical jump (Sargent chalk jump).** (See Johnson and Nelson, pp. 201-202.) (See Photo Sequence 8.1.)

   Objective: To measure the power of legs in jumping vertically.

   Equipment and materials: A yardstick, several pieces of chalk, and a smooth wall surface measuring at least 12 feet high from the floor.

   Directions: The performer should stand with one side toward a wall, heels together, and hold a 2.54-centimeter (1-in.) piece of chalk in the hand nearest to the wall. Keeping the heels on the floor, he or she reaches upward as high as possible and makes a mark on the wall. The performer then jumps as high as possible and makes another mark at the height of the jump. The use of an arm swing is allowed.

PHOTO SEQUENCE 8.1
Student taking the vertical jump test (left to right).

Scoring: The number of centimeters between the reach and jump marks measured to the nearest centimeter is the score. Three to five trials are allowed and the best trial is recorded as the score.

Additional pointers: (a) A double jump or a "crow hop" should not be permitted upon take-off; (b) the chalk should not be extended more than necessary beyond the fingertips to make the standing and jumping marks; (c) given adequate space and trained student assistants, more than one subject can be tested at one time.

Reliability: Reported as high as .93.

Objectivity: Reported to be .93.

Validity: A validity of .78 has been reported with the criterion of a sum of four track and field event scores.

Reported norms (Friermood, 1967). See Table 8.1.

2. **Shuttle run** (AAHPER, 1965).

Objective: To measure speed and change of direction.

TABLE 8.1
VERTICAL JUMP NORMS (cm)*

PERCENTILE	Sex Age	Male				Female			
		9-11	12-14	15-17	18-34	9-11	12-14	15-17	18-34
90		38	46	61	64	38	38	41	33
80		36	43	58	61	36	36	38	33
70		31	41	53	58	31	33	36	30
60		28	36	48	48	28	30	33	25
50		25	33	41	41	25	28	28	20
40		23	28	30	33	23	25	20	15
30		18	23	20	23	18	20	15	10
20		10	13	13	20	10	10	8	5
10		5	5	5	5	5	5	5	3

*Example: A 14-year-old female scored 33. Her percentile rank score would be 70.

Equipment and materials: Each station needs two blocks of wood (5 X 5 X 10 cm), a stop watch, and a 9-meter (about 30-ft) running area (width of a volleyball court).

Directions: The subject starts from a standing position behind one of the lines. Behind the other line are placed the two blocks of wood. At the starting signal the subject races to the blocks, picks one up, and runs back to the starting line. He or she places (not throws) the wooden block behind the starting line, runs back and picks up the remaining wood block, and then carries it across the starting line. In all, the distance is crossed four times, making a total distance of 36 meters. Two trials are given with some rest between trials.

Scoring: The time to the nearest tenth of a second of the better of two trials is the score for the event.

Additional pointers: (a) To facilitate testing, the runners should be divided so half start from one side and half from the other side. Starting them alternately eliminates carrying the blocks of wood back each time. (b) With additional stop watches and trained student assistants, more than one subject can be tested at a time.

Reliability, objectivity, and validity: The individual items in the AAPHER Youth Fitness Test were selected with these factors in mind, but no specific coefficients are given.

Reported norms (AAPHER, 1965). See Table 8.2.

3. **Push-ups.** (See Johnson and Nelson, pp. 128-131.)

Objective: To measure the strength and muscular endurance of the arms and shoulder girdle.

Equipment and materials: Floor mat if available.

Directions: (*Males*) From a straight-arm front-leaning rest position, the performer lowers the body until the chest touches the mat and then pushes upward to the straight-arm support.

TABLE 8.2
AAHPER SHUTTLE RUN NORMS (sec)

PERCENTILE	Sex	Male				Female			
	Age	9-11	12-14	15-17	18-22	10-11	12-14	15-17	18-22
90		10.2	9.8	9.1	9.1	10.5	10.2	10.3	10.5
80		10.5	10.0	9.3	9.2	11.0	10.6	10.6	10.9
70		10.8	10.2	9.5	9.5	11.1	10.9	10.9	11.1
60		11.0	10.4	9.7	9.6	11.5	11.2	11.0	11.3
50		11.2	10.6	9.9	9.7	11.9	11.4	11.2	11.6
40		11.5	10.8	10.0	9.9	12.0	11.7	11.5	11.9
30		11.8	11.1	10.2	10.0	12.4	12.0	11.9	12.1
20		12.0	11.5	10.6	10.2	12.8	12.5	12.2	12.4
10		12.6	12.0	11.1	10.6	13.1	13.2	13.0	12.9

PHOTO SEQUENCE 8.2
Male student executing push-ups for men and boys.

The exercise continues for as many repetitions as possible without rest. The body must not sag or pike upward but maintain a straight line throughout the exercise. (See Photo Sequence 8.2.)

   (*Females*) The women and girls do a modified push-up test. With the knees bent at right angles and the hands on the floor, the performer lowers her body to the floor until the chest touches, and then she pushes back to the starting position. The exercise is continued for as many repetitions as possible without rest. (See Photo Sequence 8.3.)

Scoring: The score is the number of correct push-ups executed.

Additional pointers: (a) The score is terminated if the performer stops to rest; (b) if the chest does not touch or if the arms are not completely extended on an execution, the trial does not count; (c) for large-group testing, the subjects perform in pairs while the instructor counts for

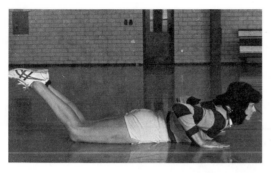

PHOTO SEQUENCE 8.3
Female student executing modified push-ups for women and girls.

the group (approximately one complete push-up per second). When a subject misses a cadence count, the test is over for that subject, and his or her partner notes the score.

Reliability: For the modified push-up test, a reliability as high as .93 has been reported.

Objectivity: A coefficient as high as .99 has been reported.

Validity: Face validity generally accepted. However, a coefficient of .72 has been reported with the Rogers Index as the criterion (Wilson, 1944).

Reported norms. (See Johnson and Nelson, pp. 238-131.) See Table 8.3.

TABLE 8.3
PUSH-UP NORMS (number)*

PERCENTILE	Sex Age	Male				Female			
		9-11	12-14	15-17	18-22	9-11	12-14	15-17	18-22
90		26	35	39	41	34	49	54	53
80		22	29	33	35	25	38	47	46
70		19	26	30	32	20	31	39	38
60		16	24	28	30	16	26	32	31
50		14	21	25	27	12	21	25	24
40		12	18	22	24	8	15	17	16
30		9	16	20	26	4	10	10	9
20		6	13	17	29	0	3	3	2
10		2	7	11	23	0	0	0	0

*The girl's and women's push-ups are of the modified variety.

The Skill Domain

For the evaluation of skill development, four tests have been selected. Each of the selected tests evaluates a specific volleyball skill (face passing, forearm passing, serving, and spiking). To expedite the evaluation, the tests should be administered at several test stations with the assistance of student leaders.

1. AAHPER face pass wall-volley test (AAHPER, 1969). (See Photo 8.4.)

PHOTO 8.4
Student taking the AAHPER face pass wall-volley test.

Objective: To measure the ability and speed with which a player can volley (face pass) a volley-ball against a wall.

Equipment and materials: A solid smooth wall with a 2.54-centimeter (1-in.) wide line marked on it which is 1.52 meters (5 ft) long, and 3.35 meters (11 ft) above and parallel to the floor. Vertical lines extending upward from each end of the line are approximately 1 meter long. In addition, a stop watch, scoring sheet, and volleyball for each test station are required.

Directions: The player with the volleyball stands facing the wall. On signal "go," the ball is tossed against the wall into the area bounded by the lines. On the rebound the ball is then volleyed consecutively for one minute. The tossed ball and each volley must strike the wall above the 1.52-meter line and between the vertical lines.

Scoring: Score is the total number of *legal* volleys executed within one minute. Tosses do not count in the score. Allow each student three trials and average the best two as the final score.

Additional pointers: (a) The scorer should be trained to recognize the difference between a legal and an illegal volley; (b) when testing children, lower the horizontal line and allow the ball to bounce once before being volleyed (develop own norms).

Reliability: Brady (1945) reported a reliability of .93. The Brady test is identical to the AAHPER test, except that the horizontal line is set at 3.5 meters (11 ft 6 in.).

Objectivity: None reported, but high due to nature of task.

Validity: Brady (1945) reported a validity coefficient of .86, using judge's rating of volleyball playing ability as the criterion.

Reported norms (AAHPER 1969). See Table 8.4.

TABLE 8.4
AAHPER FACE PASS WALL-VOLLEY TEST

PERCENTILE	Sex Age	Male				Female			
		9-11	12-14	15-17	18-22	9-11	12-14	15-17	18-22
90		19	31	41	50	13	25	35	38
80		15	26	37	48	8	17	24	27
70		12	22	34	44	5	13	19	20
60		9	19	31	41	3	10	15	16
50		7	17	28	38	2	8	12	12
40		5	14	24	35	1	6	9	9
30		3	11	20	32	1	4	7	7
20		2	8	17	28	0	2	5	5
10		0	5	12	21	0	0	3	3

2. **Brumbach forearm pass wall-volley test** (Borrevik, 1969). (See Photo 8.5.)

Objective: To measure the ability and speed with which a player can volley (forearm pass) a volleyball against a wall.

Equipment and materials: A solid smooth wall with a 2.54-centimeter (1-in.) wide line marked on it. This line is 2.44 meters (8 ft) above, and parallel to, the floor. In addition, stop watch, scoring sheet, and volleyball are required for each test station.

Directions: The player with the volleyball in hand stands facing the wall. On signal "go," the ball is tossed against the wall into the area bounded by the lines. On the rebound the ball is volleyed (forearm pass) against the wall and above the 2.44-meter line.

Scoring: Score is the total number of legal volleys executed within one minute. Each performer receives three trials. The average of the two best trials is the final score. Tosses do not count in the score.

PHOTO 8.5
Student taking the Brumbach forearm pass wall-volley test.

Additional pointers: For children, allow the ball to bounce once before being volleyed (develop own norms).

Reliability: Borrevik (1969) reported reliability as high as .896.

Objectivity: None reported, but high due to nature of task.

Validity: Cox (1977) reported a validity coefficient of .80 with passing performance in game situation as the criterion.

Reported norms (Norms developed by author). See Table 8.5.

3. **AAHPER serving accuracy test** (AAHPER, 1969).

Objective: To measure the player's skill in serving (accuracy) as in an actual game.

Equipment and materials: Volleyballs, volleyball net and standards, court marked as indicated in Figure 8.1.

Directions: Server X (see Figure 8.1) stands opposite the marked court in the proper serving position. The server may use any legal serve in hitting the ball over into the opposite court. For children below the age of twelve, the serving line should be located 20 feet from the net.

Scoring: The server is given ten trials. When the ball hits the net and does or does not go over, it counts as a trial but no points are given. The score is the total number of points made. Points are determined by where the ball lands in the opposite court (see Figure 8.1). For balls that strike on a line, the higher score of the areas concerned is awarded.

TABLE 8.5
BRUMBACH FOREARM PASS WALL-VOLLEY TEST

PERCENTILE	Sex Age	Male				Female			
		9-11	12-14	15-17	18-22	9-11	12-14	15-17	18-22
90		17	23	32	48	17	23	41	44
80		13	19	28	42	13	19	34	37
70		10	16	25	39	10	16	30	33
60		8	14	23	37	8	14	27	29
50		6	12	21	34	6	12	24	26
40		4	10	19	31	4	10	21	23
30		2	8	17	29	2	8	18	19
20		0	5	14	26	0	5	14	15
10		0	1	10	20	0	1	7	10

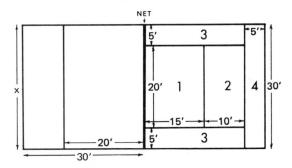

FIGURE 8.1

Additional pointers: It is recommended that the server be restricted to the area behind the serving line that is within 10 feet (about 3 m) of the right sideline. This minor modification will make the test conform to current USVBA, NFSHSA, and NAGWS rules.

Reliability, objectivity and validity: The AAHPER serving test was developed with these factors in mind but no specific coefficients are given.

Reported norms (AAHPER, 1969). See Table 8.6.

4. **Stanley spike test** (Stanley, 1967). (See Photo 8.6.)

Objective: To measure volleyball spiking ability.

Equipment and materials: A smooth wall, a restraining line marked on the floor 4.57 meters (15 ft) from the wall, a ball, scoresheet, and stop watch.

Directions: Subject starts behind, and must remain behind, the restraining line. The test begins with the subject throwing the ball up and hitting it into the floor so that it bounces back (see

TABLE 8.6
AAHPER SERVING TEST

PERCENTILE	Sex Age	Male				Female			
		9-11	12-14	15-17	18-22	9-11	12-14	15-17	18-22
90		27	29	33	33	20	24	26	26
80		23	26	30	31	16	19	22	23
70		21	23	29	30	14	16	20	20
60		18	21	26	27	12	14	17	18
50		16	19	23	24	10	12	15	16
40		14	17	21	21	8	9	13	14
30		12	15	19	19	6	7	12	13
20		9	12	15	16	4	5	9	10
10		7	8	12	12	10	2	6	7

PHOTO 8.6
Student taking the Stanley wall-volley spike test.

Figure 5.12). The subject must continue floor-to-wall volley by jumping and hitting the ball into the floor. The subject does not jump to start the test.

Scoring: Score for a single trial is the total number of spikes completed in 60 seconds. Final score is the average of two trials. The hit that starts each rally does not count in the score.

Additional pointers: The spiker must be in the air when he or she strikes the ball and the ball must be at least above chest height when hit.

Reliability: Correlation coefficient of .80 reported by Stanley (1967).

Objectivity: Correlation of .98 reported by Stanley.

Validity: Correlation of .64 reported by Stanley. Criterion of performance was judges' ratings (two) of actual spiking ability.

Reported norms (Norms developed by author). See Table 8.7.

TABLE 8.7
STANLEY SPIKE TEST

PERCENTILE	Sex Age	Male				Female			
		9-11	12-14	15-17	18-22	9-11	12-24	15-17	18-22
90		12	16	19	20	12	16	19	20
80		10	14	16	18	10	14	16	18
70		8	12	14	16	8	12	14	16
60		7	11	12	14	7	11	12	14
50		6	10	11	12	6	10	11	12
40		5	9	10	10	5	9	10	10
30		4	8	8	8	4	8	8	8
20		2	6	6	6	2	6	6	6
10		0	4	3	4	0	4	3	4

The Cognitive Domain

The primary consideration here is the evaluation of knowledge acquisition. In the Suggested Student Projects sections of chapters 5, 6, and 7, it was recommended that true-false and multiple-choice test questions be composed on the material contained in those chapters. The same questions can be used for evaluation of knowledge acquisition. The student is also referred to the section on measurement of knowledge in Johnson and Nelson (pp. 408-420) for assistance in writing knowledge questions.

The Affective Domain

As explained in chapter 2, the affective domain relates to our feelings, attitudes, values, and motives. A number of worthwhile scales for measuring development in the affective domain have been developed (Adams, 1963; Kenyon, 1968; Mercer, 1971; Richardson, 1960; and Wear, 1955). In this book, only the Kenyon Attitude Scale will be presented.

The stated purpose of the Kenyon Scale is to measure attitude toward the multidimensional domain of physical activity. The Kenyon test is based upon a six-dimensional model of physical activity. The men's (boys') scale consists of 59 statements, while the women's (girls') consists of 54 statements. The respondent's attitude toward a statement is scored on a seven-point scale, ranging from *very strongly disagree* to *very strongly agree*.

The subject's score on each dimension (social experience, health and fitness, pursuit of vertigo, aesthetic experience, catharsis, and ascetic experience) is the sum of the homogeneous items associated with each of the six factors. The total of all six factors should not be summed. A description of each dimension is given in Table 8.8.

TABLE 8.8
DIMENSIONS OF THE KENYON ATTITUDE SCALE*

DIMENSION NUMBER	DIMENSION NAME	DIMENSION DESCRIPTION
I	Physical activity as a social experience	Individuals who score high on this factor value physical activities that provide a medium for social interaction.
II	Physical activity for health and fitness	Individuals who score high on this factor value physical activity for its contribution to health and fitness.
III	Physical activity as the pursuit of vertigo	Individuals who score high on this factor value physical activity that provides an element of thrill at some risk to the participant.
IV	Physical activity as an aesthetic experience	Individuals who score high on this factor perceive physical activity as having aesthetic value (activity perceived as possessing beauty or artistic qualities).
V	Physical activity as catharsis	Individuals who score high on this factor perceive physical activity as providing a release from frustration and pressures of modern living.
VI	Physical activity as an ascetic experience	Individuals who score high on this factor value the type of dedication involved for championship-level performance (hard work and dedication).

*Reliability coefficients for the six dimensions are provided by Kenyon (1968).

The full Kenyon Attitude Scale adapted both for men and boys and for women and girls is provided in numerous measurement-and-evaluation textbooks for physical education (see Baumgartner and Jackson, pp. 253-264). The Kenyon Scale should be used sparingly. For example, it would be inappropriate to administer it more than once to the same group of students in a given year.

Conversely, it might be extremely useful to compare student scores on selected dimensions from the beginning of one school year to the next. The effect of volleyball participation on attitudes might be ascertained by comparing the scores of students electing to take volleyball with the scores of students who elect to take other activities.

The Personal-Social Domain

The personal-social domain relates to the manner in which physical activity and sports participation promote the development of leadership, sportsmanship, and self-confidence. For the measurement of these various factors, four tests are recommended. Unlike the Kenyon attitude test, these simple-to-administer tests may be utilized two or three times a year (or even before and after a volleyball unit).

1. Blanchard behavioral rating scale (Blanchard, 1946). The objective of this test is to measure the character and personality of students. For details of the test, see Johnson and Nelson, p. 391.

2. Breck's sociometric test of status (Breck, 1950). The objective of this test is to measure the status of students within a group. For details of this test, see Johnson and Nelson, pp. 392-393.

3. Volleyball sportsmanship attitude scale (Johnson, 1969). The purpose of this test is to evaluate sportsmanship attitudes. Details are found in Johnson and Nelson, pp. 402-403. To make the test more appropriate for volleyball players, I have constructed the scale shown in Table 8.9. This scale should be used in conjunction with the Johnson and Nelson guidelines.

TABLE 8.9
VOLLEYBALL SPORTSMANSHIP ATTITUDE SCALE

QUESTION	RESPONSE			
	1	2	3	4
1. After a volleyball player was called for lifting, he/she slammed the volleyball onto the floor.				
2. After a technical foul was called against a volleyball player, he/she shook his/her fist at the referee.				
3. A member of one team was continually using abusive language against members of the opposing team.				
4. After a volleyball match the coach of the losing team went up to the referee and demanded to know how much money had been paid to "throw" the game.				
5. Members of one team were consistently and purposely attempting to screen the opposing team's view of the serve.				
6. A blocker who last touched a ball that was hit out of bounds by the opposing team's spiker yells "no touch."				
7. As the volleyball coach left the gymnasium after the game, he/she shouted at the referee, "I never saw such lousy officiating in my life."				

TABLE 8.9 (continued)

QUESTION	RESPONSE 1 2 3 4
8. The team captain, after being called for a double hit on serve reception, informs the referee that he/she was in error, and a replay should be called.	
9. In a particularly close game, the server rubbed the ball on his/her sweaty jersey to increase the chances of a "mishandle" by the opposing team's setter.	
10. The team captain of one team contested virtually every call made by the referee against his/her team.	
11. After being ejected from a match for unsportsmanlike conduct, the ejected player informed the referee that he/she would "get" him/her after the match.	
12. One member of a losing team, realizing his/her team had no more time outs, faked an injury to get the referee to stop the game for a few minutes.	
13. Following a closely played volleyball match, the coach of the losing team cursed his/her players for not winning.	
14. During a time-out in a volleyball game, the timer accidentally left the 8-minute clock running. The coach whose team was behind accused the timer of purposely trying to influence the result of the game.	
15. The captain of the protesting team shoved the linesman, when the linesman called a ball "in" that the captain was sure was "out."	
16. Spectators sitting directly behind the referee shouted "throw" or "double hit" every time the setter of the team they opposed handled the ball.	
17. To camouflage the fact that a back-row player of Team A had illegally blocked for a point, the captain of Team A called a time-out.	
18. After being called for mishandling the ball on a set, the penalized player kicked the volleyball into the stands.	
19. In an effort to stall for time, the captain of one team repeatedly asked for a towel to wipe up wet spots on the floor.	
20. In a show of disrespect, the captain of the offending team turns his back on the referee when the referee attempts to explain a ruling.	

4. **Volleyball leadership questionnaire** (Nelson, 1966). The objective of this test is to identify team leaders as identified by team members. The details for test administration may be found in Johnson and Nelson, pp. 393-395. To make the test more appropriate for volleyball players, I have constructed the questionnaire displayed in Table 8.10. This questionnaire should be used in conjunction with the Johnson and Nelson guidelines.

TABLE 8.10
VOLLEYBALL LEADERSHIP QUESTIONNAIRE

QUESTIONS	PLAYERS NAMES	
	A	B
1. Who are the most popular members of your squad or class?		
2. Who are the best scholars of your squad or class?		
3. Which players know the most about the game of volleyball?		
4. If the teacher (coach) were not present, which players would you prefer to take charge of the instruction?		
5. If the teacher (coach) were not present, which players would most likely take charge of the situation?		
6. Which members of your squad or class are the other students most likely to listen to when your team is in need of inspiration?		
7. Which members of your squad or class exhibit the most poise during crucial parts of a match?		
8. Who are the most valuable members of the squad or class?		
9. Which members of your squad or class have most favorably influenced you?		
10. Which teammates do you think would make the best coaches?		
11. Which teammates do you often look to for leadership?		
12. Which members of your squad or class do you think exhibit the greatest amount of leadership ability?		

SUGGESTED STUDENT PROJECTS

1. Administer the vertical jump test to several of your classmates (your instructor might have other members of the class practice administering the other three physical fitness tests). How do your classmates compare with the norms in Tables 8.1, 8.2, and 8.3?

2. Utilizing the intent in project 1, administer the Brumbach wall-volley test to several of your classmates. Again, how do your classmates' norms compare with the norms in Tables 8.4 through 8.7?

3. Volunteer your services to assist a practicing (college, YMCA, high school, etc.) teacher in the administration of selected skill tests. Using the data gathered from this project, develop a table of norms for each test administered.

4. Go to the library and look up the Kenyon Physical Activity Scale. Self-administer the test. How do the results compare with your feelings about your attitudes? Which dimensions of the test do you like the best? Would you administer this test to your students?

5. Estimate percentile scores for the student scores listed below:

Sex	Age	Vertical Jump Test	Shuttle Run Test	AAHPER Serve Test	Brumbach Passing Test
M	10	35 cm	10 sec	20	6
F	11	24 cm	11 sec	4	17
M	13	45 cm	12 sec	10	5
F	14	9 cm	10 sec	15	10
M	16	59 cm	11 sec	31	31
F	17	20 cm	10 sec	25	35
M	19	65 cm	9 sec	15	40
F	34	8 cm	12 sec	8	45

6. Use several measurement-and-evaluation books in physical education to look up the following personal-social tests: (a) Blanchard behavioral rating scale, (b) Breck's sociometric test of status, (c) the Johnson sportsmanship attitude scale, and (d) the Nelson leadership questionnaire. Take notes on the administrative procedures of each test. Self-administer two of these tests. Would you use these tests in your instruction? Why?

REFERENCES

AAHPER. *Volleyball Skills Test Manual.* Washington, D.C.: American Association for Health, Physical Education and Recreation, 1969.

AAHPER. *Youth Fitness Test Manual.* Rev. ed. Washington, D.C.: American Association for Health, Physical Education and Recreation, 1965.

Adams, R.S. "Two Scales for Measuring Attitude toward Physical Education." *Research Quarterly,* 34 (1963), 91-94.

Barrow, H.M., and R. McGee. *A Practical Approach to Measurement in Physical Education.* 2nd ed. Philadelphia: Lea and Febiger, 1971.

Baumgartner, T.A., and A.S. Jackson. *Measurement for Evaluation in Physical Education.* Boston: Houghton Mifflin Co., 1975.

Blanchard, B.E. "A Comparative Analysis of Secondary School Boys' and Girls' Character and Personality Traits in Physical Education Classes." *Research Quarterly,* 17 (1946), 33-39.

Borrevik, B.A. "A Study to Evaluate Two Volleyball Forearm Volley Tests for College Men." Unpublished paper, University of Oregon, 1969.

Brady, G.F. "Preliminary Investigations of Volleyball Playing Ability." *Research Quarterly,* 16 (1945), 14-17.

Breck, S.J. "A Sociometric Measurement of Status in Physical Education Classes." *Research Quarterly,* 21 (1950), 75-82.

Cowell, C.C. "Validating an Index of Social Adjustment for High School Use." *Research Quarterly*, 29 (1958), 7-18.

Cox, R.H. "Validity of Brumbach Forearm Passing Test for Volleyball." Paper presented at the Research Section of the 1977 KAHPER Convention, Topeka, Kansas.

Friermood, H.T. "Volleyball Skills Contest for Olympic Development." In *USVBA Official Volleyball Rules and Reference Guide.* Berne, Indiana: United States Volleyball Association Printer, 1967.

Johnson, B.L., and J.K. Nelson. *Practical Measurements for Evaluation in Physical Education.* 3rd ed. Minneapolis: Burgess Publishing Co., 1979.

Johnson, M.L. "Construction of Sportsmanship Attitude Scales." *Research Quarterly,* 40 (1969), 312-316.

Kenyon, G.S. "Six Scales for Assessing Attitude toward Physical Activity." *Research Quarterly,* 39 (1968), 566-574.

Mercer, E.L. "Mercer Attitude Scale." In *A Practical Approach to Measurement,* ed. H.M. Barrow and R. McGee. Philadelphia: Lea and Febiger, 1971. pp. 431-434.

Nelson, D.O. "Leadership in Sports." *Research Quarterly,* 37 (1966), 268-275.

Richardson, C.E. "Thurston Scale for Measuring Attitudes of College Students towards Physical Fitness and Exercise. *Research Quarterly,* 31 (1960), 635-643.

Stanley, J. "A Volleyball Spike Skill Test for College Men." Master's thesis. Brigham Young University, Provo, Utah, 1967.

Wear, C.L. "The Evaluation of Attitude toward Physical Activity as an Activity Course." *Research Quarterly,* 22 (1951), 114-126.

Wilson, M. "Study of Arm and Shoulder Girdle Strength of College Women in Selected Tests." *Research Quarterly,* 15 (1944), 258.

Coaching Tips

The volleyball coach is a teacher. In fact, success as a coach will depend to a great extent upon teaching ability. The coach, however, has additional practical concerns that are generated from competition, such as training and conditioning, practice sessions, scheduling, and team selection processes. Several of these "coaching" concerns will be briefly discussed here and a number of hints for dealing with them effectively will be identified.

TRAINING AND CONDITIONING

In any given volleyball match, all other things being equal, the team in the best physical condition will be victorious. It therefore behooves the volleyball coach to help his or her team get in top condition. Aspects of physical fitness that are especially important to volleyball players are flexibility, strength, muscular endurance, cardiovascular endurance (anaerobic as opposed to aerobic), quickness, and leg power. Opportunities for the development of volleyball fitness can be divided into three parts: preseason training, pre-competition season training, and competition season training.

Preseason Training

Preseason training is training that the athlete does on his or her own during the off season. It should commence at least six weeks prior to the first practice of the year. The athlete should receive specific instructions concerning the type of training from the volleyball coach. In addition, each athlete should fulfill specific objectives before reporting to practice. Suggested training activities and specific goals are listed in Box 9.1. On the first day of practice, each returning player should be tested and specific performance expectations adjusted according to age, sex, and skill-level differences. Each player should also report to practice with a recent physical examination administered by a medical doctor, and athletes who have difficulty in keeping trim should be encouraged to maintain an "ideal" weight.

Pre-Competition Season Training

Since all athletes do not report the first day of practice in top physical condition, the first part of the volleyball season is often devoted to conditioning. This is only acceptable if the season is four

BOX 9.1.
SUGGESTED PRE-SEASON CONDITIONING PROGRAM AND GOALS TO BE MET

ACTIVITY	GOALS
1. Run one mile.	1. Seven-minute mile for girls and women, and 6.5-minute mile for boys and men.
2. Push-ups.	2. Thirty push-ups (modified for girls and women).
3. Sit-ups.	3. Fifty bent-knee sit-ups.
4. Forward dives.	4. Twenty forward dives (2 sets of 10 with 2-minute rest between sets).
5. Japanese rolls.	5. Twenty rolls (10 to each side).
6. Wind sprints.	6. Run six 50-yard wind sprints with 2-minute rest between.
7. Mock volleyball approach and jump for spike.	7. Three sets of 10 maximum-effort repetitions.
8. Mock blocking drill against wall (see Figure 5.14).	8. Three sets of 10 maximum-effort repetitions.
9. Barbell leg squats (if available).	9. One set of 50 repetitions with 50% body weight for females and 75% body weight for males. (Note: Do not flex knees beyond a 90° angle, keep back straight and eyes forward.)

months long, and the athletes have six weeks to get in shape before the first match. However, many organizations do not have this luxury. For example, most high school and college women's programs begin their season when school starts in the fall, the first match often falling within three weeks of the first day of practice. Consequently, as a coach, you cannot afford to sacrifice skill and knowledge of team tactics for fitness. Your pre-competition season training must incorporate both skill and fitness development, and many of the drills selected for skill development must also be selected for conditioning purposes.

Most of the drills diagrammed in chapters 5, 6, and 7 may be adapted for both skill and fitness purposes. To assist the coach in fitness development, the following fitness-related skill drills are presented.

1. Organized service reception drill for 12 to 15 athletes. (See Figure 9.1.) Each person serves 30 balls to the receiver (#1) in the opposite court. The receiver receives 15 balls from each of two deep receiving positions and bumps balls to the setter (#2). The setter back sets to a person in the off-hand spiking position (#3), who relays the ball back to the feeder (#4). The feeder feeds balls to the server (#5), who serves as rapidly as possible. Extra players (#6) act as shaggers to keep wayward balls in circulation. Servers must be accurate if drill is to operate efficiently. Since both sides are working in unison, the sides are working as mirror images of each other. Players rotate after thirty serves.

2. Spike digging drill. (See Figure 9.2.) Two players position themselves 2 meters (about 7 ft) from the baseline and 3 meters (about 10 ft) from each other while facing the net. The coach (C) stands within one meter of the net and hits hard-driven spikes and dinks at the diggers (D). This is done in a rapid-fire manner with the diggers changing positions after fifteen dig attempts at the starting position. Players (S) waiting to take their turn should be shagging loose balls and feeding them to the coach. (*Note:* Two drills can be run simultaneously on each side of a single net.)

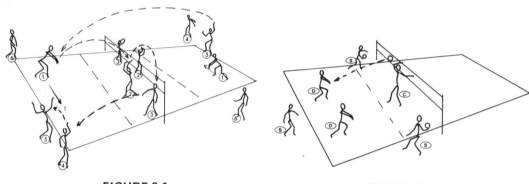

FIGURE 9.1   **FIGURE 9.2**

3. Organized large-group diving drill for technique and conditioning. (See Figure 9.3.) Athletes line up behind the baseline and face the net in three lines (D). The coach (C) is positioned at the net and shaggers (S) are distributed around the court. The divers at the head of each line dive for balls thrown in front of them. After each diving save attempt, the athlete moves to the end of another line. Drill continues until each athlete has dived for thirty balls in rapid succession.

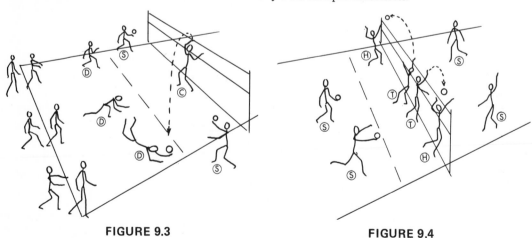

FIGURE 9.3   **FIGURE 9.4**

4. Spiking drill for conditioning. (See Figure 9.4.) Hitter (H) spikes twenty balls on-hand and off-hand. After each spike attempt, the hitter drops back to the 3-meter line and immediately attacks again. Sets are lofted into the air, one meter above the net by the tossers (T) in rapid succession. Shaggers (S) are kept busy returning balls to the tossers. After hitting ten balls on-hand, the hitter takes a brief rest and then hits ten balls off-hand (or vice versa).

Competition Season Training

Many coaches think that once the competitive season starts, the athletes will play themselves into top physical condition. But this is simply not true. It is very difficult to stay in top condition just playing matches and tournaments—and this is especially true for the reserves.

To ensure that all of the athletes maintain an acceptable level of fitness, it is necessary to conduct at least one non-skill-related conditioning drill during each practice session. This conditioning drill should be administered at or near the end of the practice session. To make the drills interesting, they should be varied from practice to practice. To be most beneficial, the drill should involve running or jumping and be anaerobic in nature.

Conditioning drills may be selected from the following list.

1. Wind sprints. Have athletes run as hard as they can for 18 meters (about 60 ft), rest for 60 seconds, and run another 18 meters. Run as many sprints as necessary to ensure that the athletes are fatigued (6 to 10 repetitions are recommended).

2. Block and diving drill (no ball). The athlete begins the drill in a blocking position at the net. On the signal to start, he or she executes a maximum-effort block (vertical jump), recovers from the block, turns and executes a forward dive in the direction of the baseline, recovers from the dive, and then sprints to the net. This cycle continues until each athlete has completed 10 blocks and 20 dives. The entire drill may be repeated if necessary.

3. Spike approach and vertical jump drill. Athletes execute a mock spike approach and jump 30 times. This should be done in 6 sets of 5 jumps per set. After each set of five jumps, the athlete receives a 60-second rest. The 60 seconds can be used to return the athletes to a common starting point. A maximum effort from each athlete is expected.

4. Lateral-movement blocking drill. Athletes take a position close to a net or a flat wall so that they have four meters of space to work with. Upon command, the athlete executes a mock block against the wall (or net), recovers from the block and executes a 3-meter lateral movement to his or her left, again executes the mock block, recovers and executes a 3-meter lateral movement to his or her right, and again executes a mock block. This continues until the athlete has jumped fifteen times in rapid succession. Allowing a 2-minute rest between sets of fifteen jumps, repeat three times for a total of 45 jumps. See Figures 5.21 and 7.10 for clarification and methods for moving laterally.

5. Jumping the bleacher seats. (See Photo 9.1.) Utilizing a deep crouch and maximum-effort vertical jump, have athletes jump bleacher seats. For example, if the bleachers are ten seats high (1 set), require 10 sets with a 30-second rest between sets. For safety, do not jump bleachers that are not permanent or that would allow a person to fall between the steps.

THE PRACTICE SESSION

There are a number of variables to consider in organizing daily practice sessions. These variables will be discussed in this section under the headings of (a) seasonal practice progression, (b) daily practice preparations, and (c) daily practice progression.

PHOTO 9.1.
Athlete in a deep crouch for jumping a set of bleacher seats.

Seasonal Practice Progression

Seasonal volleyball practices may be divided into three parts (early, mid, and late season).

Early-season practices. This is a period of time that must be used to teach fundamental skills and team tactics. It is extremely important that all new and returning athletes be soundly instructed in terms of the proper techniques for executing individual volleyball skills (passing, setting, spiking, blocking, etc.). It is equally important that the new members of the team be familiarized with the offensive and defensive systems that have been adopted.

Mid-season practices. It is during this period of the season that team practices should be subject to periodic analysis and evaluation. Based upon the performance of the team in several competitive outings, the coach should have a good idea of the strengths and weaknesses of the team. Mid-season is a time to make the necessary adjustments in tactics and starting line-up that will either maintain performance or get the team turned around (winning instead of losing). It is also a good time to help individual players improve their personal performances.

Late-season practices. At this point in the season, it is too late to be making any major changes in team tactics or even in starting line-ups. This is a time to emphasize individual excellence. Drills and practices should emphasize the refining of the fundamental skills of the game.

Daily Practice Preparations

Plan and prepare for each practice session so as not to waste valuable practice time.

Nets. Arrange to have the nets put up at least a half hour before practice begins. Many athletes will want to come early and practice skills in which they are deficient. They cannot do this if the facility is not prepared or if they must use valuable practice time to put the nets up themselves.

Balls. As with the nets, the volleyballs should be available for use at least a half hour before practice begins. There should be enough volleyballs available for each athlete to have a ball. (The bare minimum should be one ball for each two athletes.) Select high-quality volleyballs that are likely to be used at your competitive matches (see Table 4.2). Do not practice (or play) with over-inflated volleyballs. Generally speaking, about one pound of pressure less than recommended on the ball is suggested (most volleyballs are too hard at recommended pressure).

Floors. Arrange to have the playing floors swept before practicing on them. Due to the amount of floor work (diving and rolling) that should be done, it is important to keep the floors clean. This is important not only for reasons of cleanliness but for safety as well (to prevent slipping).

Daily Practice Progression

The exact nature of daily practices will necessarily vary from day to day. For example, if the team demonstrated a weakness in service reception during the last competitive outing, then emphasize passing drills. But even though the areas of emphasis will change, the basic format of each practice will remain the same. The length of practice sessions should vary from 1½ to 2½ hours, with the average being two hours. A suggested daily practice format is presented in Box 9.2.

STATISTICAL CHARTING PROCEDURES

There are a number of reasons for statistical charting, three of the most obvious being (a) scouting the opposition, (b) determining the strengths and weaknesses of your own players for purposes of team improvement, and (c) determining strengths and weaknesses of your own players for selecting starting line-ups.

In this section three basic techniques for charting performance are discussed. The first will be called the Dunphy (1977) method; the second, an accumulative method; and the third, the error (Scates, 1976) method.

The Dunphy Method

The Dunphy method of statistical charting is used for evaluation of player passing (service reception) and spiking effectiveness. The strength of the system is that it allows for immediate analysis (e.g., during time-outs and between games). Further, it identifies the net position from which the ball is spiked as well as the direction of hit. Its weakness is that it only allows for the charting of spike effectiveness on the service reception. After this point, the complexities of the game (e.g., defensive and offensive switching) surpass the sophistication of this charting system.

Illustrated in Figure 9.5 is (a) a scouting report form for six rotations, (b) an analysis of passing and spiking in a single rotational position (one of the six), and (c) a performance key. Utilizing the performance key in Figure 9.5c, we can interpret the charted performance in Figure 9.5b. For example, in terms of passing performance we can see that the back-row receivers (3 and 2) are receiving most of the balls (as they should). We can also observe that player 3 is passing very well, while player 2 is having problems. In terms of spiking performance, each spiker (4, 5, and 6) has hit three balls on service reception (a good balance). Player 4 was effective with two spikes down the line but was blocked in a cross-court attempt. Player 5 hit a ball out of bounds and dinked twice (one dink was unsuccessful and the other was dug). Player 6 was effective with a cross-court spike, got dug with a down-the-line attempt, and hit a third attempt into the net.

BOX 9.2.
DAILY PRACTICE FORMAT

A. Team warm-up

1. Stretching (5 min).
2. Jog around floor (5 times).
3. Push-ups (10 times).
4. Sit-ups (10 times).
5. Backward somersaults (10 over each shoulder).
6. Vertical jumps (10 times).

B. Practice of fundamental skills

1. Forearm passing in pairs (200 times).
2. Face passing in pairs (200 times).
3. Pepper drill in pairs (10 minutes).

C. Practice of net skills

1. Basic spiking drills.
2. Basic spiking and blocking drills.

D. Serving and receiving drills

1. Serving back and forth.
2. Organized individual receiving drills.
3. Team receiving drills.

E. Floor drills

1. Japanese roll practice.
2. Forward dive practice.

F. Team tactics

1. Offensive team aspects.
2. Defensive team aspects.
3. Transitional aspects (offense to defense, etc.)

G. Team scrimmage

1. Controlled scrimmages.
2. Actual scored matches.

H. Team conditioning session

I. Shower

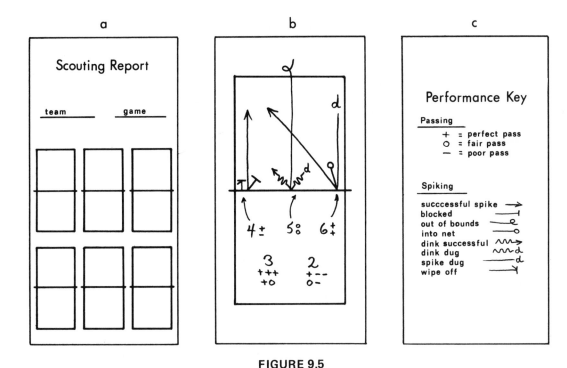

FIGURE 9.5

The Accumulative Method

In the accumulative method, skill performance may be charted for any number of skills. For the sake of simplicity, we will consider only the charting of passing (serve reception), serving, and spiking. The great advantage of this sytem is that you can get a good picture of a player's performance across an entire season, tournament, match, or game. The disadvantage is that little is learned of the specifics of a particular skill performance in terms of the direction of spike attempt, position ball was received from, etc.

In general, as indicated in Table 9.1, each player's performance for the three skills charted is recorded as being perfect (+), fair (0), or poor (-). In accumulating a player's performance for a single match, divide the total number of attempts into the number of observations per rating. For example, in ascertaining the passing effectiveness of player 1, we note the following:

Number of attempts   15
Number of +'s   6
Number of 0's   6
Number of -'s   3
Percentage of +'s = 6/15   40%
Percentage of 0's = 6/15   40%
Percentage of -'s = 3/15   20%

This would indicate that the passing performance is very poor (75% +'s is an ideal goal). In evaluating serving effectiveness, it is important to note that performance is based upon how the opposition

TABLE 9.1
CHARTING VOLLEYBALL PERFORMANCE

Team _____   Game _____

PLAYERS	SPIKING			PASSING	SERVING
	On-hand	Center	Off-hand		
1					
2					
3					
4					
5					
6					
7					
8					

handles the serve. (For example, if the serve is handled easily by the opposition, the server gets a minus).

The Error Method

Technically, all volleyball skills can be statistically charted in terms of performance (using a variation of the accumulative method), yet some of them are more difficult to chart than others. For example, it is very difficult to assess individual blocking performance using standard charting procedures. It is clear, for example, that a block for a point is good. But, is it good if the blocker does not even touch the ball? Sometimes the answer is yes, sometimes no. For example, if the blocker forces the spiker to hit the ball to a positioned digger, it must be considered good. As can be readily seen, the charting of individual performance in blocking is highly subjective. A simpler method for charting blocking performance would be to keep track of blocking errors (net violations, foot faults, etc.). After all, it is this kind of error that demoralizes and hurts a team the most. A player committing more than two blocking errors per game might have to be taken out of the game. This player obviously needs additional coaching and blocking experience.

TEAM SELECTION PROCESS

One of the questions that is often asked by beginning coaches is "Do you have any ideas for making team selection (cutting) an easier process?" It seems that no one enjoys this touchy aspect of coaching. One good answer to that question is "Don't cut!" However, even the most sympathetic of coaches has to admit that there are times when cutting is necessary (e.g., a scarcity of facilities, trained coaches, or practice time).

If player elimination is absolutely necessary, the following five steps will be helpful:

1. Make practices tough. If 60 athletes come out for the team, and only 15 can remain, find out early which ones are willing to "pay the price." If practices are sufficiently difficult, those that are out of shape or are unwilling to get in shape will drop out on their own. This strategy should result in reducing a group of 60 to 45 or less. However, for purposes of fairness the coach should make training and conditioning expectations clear to all prospective participants well in advance of the first try-out date. In addition, those who could not have known about the training requirements (new students, etc.) should be given due consideration and encouragement.

2. Administer selected (skill-related) physical fitness tests. The fitness tests described in chapter 8 are suggested. Sum the scores on the tests administered and use the summed scores as an index of fitness. Calculate a mean and a standard deviation. Athletes scoring below the 30th percentile (see chapter 8) can be cut from the squad. This would bring a group of 45 down to approximately 30 athletes. Administer these tests during the first three days of practice.

3. Administer selected volleyball skill tests. The skill tests described in chapter 8 are recommended. Again, sum the scores on the tests administered and use the summed scores as an index of skill. Calculate a mean and a standard deviation. Athletes scoring below the 20th percentile can be cut from the squad. This should bring a group of 30 athletes down to about 24. Administer these tests during the first three days of practice also.

4. Observe performance in game situation. For purposes of practice and team selection, organize a series of practice scrimmages among your remaining players. Unobtrusively, keep statistics on passing, serving, and spiking. Do not require players to use newly learned team tactics (especially if they are complex). This will allow new players to perform without fear of being "lost" on the court. Athletes with the best combined performance scores should be the best volleyball players. Make sure that each athlete has had a fair chance to perform each skill many times (for example, 50 serves, spikes, and passes). This phase should last one or two weeks and should bring the squad down to 17 or 18.

5. Consider special team needs. Base the final selection of players (from 17 to 15) on the special needs of the team. What do you need most, a setter or a spiker? A tough server or a good passer?

SCHEDULING TOURNAMENTS AND MATCHES

Dual matches are usually scheduled in conjunction with an organized league. The league officers will consider, of course, such factors as playing site, time of contest, and traveling distance. The main thing is to make sure that the officers are aware of special requests or problems that your team might have (adequacy of home facility, traveling distance, conflict with important school or city events).

The organizing and scheduling of a tournament, on the other hand, is relatively complex and involves a great deal of planning. For example, if the tournament is to be a sanctioned USVBA tournament, then the Regional Commissioner of USVBA volleyball must be contacted. For convenience, the steps for hosting and organizing a volleyball tournament are outlined in Table 9.2.

TABLE 9.2
STEPS FOR ORGANIZING A VOLLEYBALL TOURNAMENT

STEPS	TIME IN ADVANCE
1. Identify an ideal and one alternative date for hosting the tournament.	4 months
2. Identify a facility for housing the tournament.	4 months
3. If selected dates are acceptable, reserve the facility for both the ideal and the alternative dates.	4 months
4. Write a letter to the regional commissioner of volleyball or the head of the governing body under whose auspices the tournament will be held and request that either your first or second date be placed on the list of planned tournaments.	3½ months
5. Confirm your playing facility and date with the appropriate people.	3 months
6. Obtain a mailing list of the teams that are to be invited to the tournament.	2½ months
7. Consult the governing body official rule book for guidelines for obtaining sanctioning (USVBA, NFSHSA, or AIAW).	2 months
8. Send letters of invitation to invited teams. Specify date, starting time, playing site, type of tournament, sex, level of play, entrance fee, and deadline for receiving entries.	1½ months
9. Order necessary plaques, trophies, and awards for the tournament.	1½ months
10. Begin process of selecting and training tournament director, court managers, scorers, timers, linespeople, and officials.	1 month
11. Send each entered team a playing schedule, list of motels, list of restaurants, directions to playing site, and time of pregame coach's meeting.	2 weeks
12. Confirm the selection and training of court managers, scorers, timers, linespeople, and officials.	2 weeks
13. Set up standards, nets, antennae, scorer's tables, referee stands, and bleachers.	night before
14. Host a pretournament coaches' meeting to explain details of tournament and special house rules.	1 hour
15. Host the "winner's circle" for presentation of trophies, awards, and pictures.	right after

COACHING PHILOSOPHY

What type of coach are you? Do you embrace a particular philosophy of coaching? What do you see as your prime function as a coach? How important is winning to you? How do you value the athletic experience aside from winning or losing? These are some questions that prospective volleyball coaches ought to ask themselves in order to develop an overall perspective on their coaching role.

Although it is not my intention to suggest an "ideal" philosophy of coaching, the following guidelines might prove useful. For example, in terms of emphasis upon winning, a philosophy might be represented on a continuum. At one end of the continuum, we can find the philosophy that values winning above all else. At the other extreme, we find a coaching philosophy that values player participation above team success. A sound coaching philosophy would incorporate the best of both and settle for a sensible compromise.

The coach who values winning above all else cannot afford to allow a nonstarter to be on the court. The chance that the reserve player might make a critical mistake is too great. Consequently, only six players are rewarded for the hours of practice they put in. Unless there is a great deal of incentive to remain on the team, this coach may find himself or herself with only six players by the end of the season!

The coach who values participation above winning allows all twelve of his or her players to play in every contest regardless of outcome. Although at first glance this coach would appear to be a respected coach, such is not always the case. This coach may also wind up with only six players on the team, because the six best players will look elsewhere for motivating competition.

In most cases coaching philosophy that falls between these two extremes is best. The coach needs to value winning because that is the objective of the game. However, he or she must also consider team morale, player development, and social interaction as important objectives for the athletic experience. This is especially true for the coach who is also an educator. The educator must look upon the athletic experience as a developmental tool, admittedly difficult to do, especially if there is a great deal of sponsorship pressure to produce a winner. It is for this reason that the coach must have a sensible and well-developed philosophy.

If the coaching situation is associated with young people in public or private school (junior and senior high school), the coach must also consider the role of parents. Collectively, the parents of young people should have a say in the quality of the athletic programs in their schools. The appropriate forum for this input is the local school board and various parent-teacher associations. However, at no time should a coach tolerate a small group of parents (or even one parent) to dictate their own personal desires to the group.

From a more practical standpoint, parents should be thoroughly informed of the activities of the athletic program in which their child participates. They should be encouraged to attend contests, help athletes keep training rules, and support their child with personal encouragement.

ADVANCED TACTICS

Generally speaking, the team tactics introduced in chapters 5, 6, and 7 are more than sufficient for most coaching situations. However, for the coach who is associated with an accelerated program and highly skilled athletes, this may not be true. For this reason, three additional concepts will be briefly discussed.

Alternate Receiving Formations

Throughout the text, the W-formation has been emphasized. There is one situation, however, in which an alternative formation might be more desirable (see Figure 7.16b_2). This situation occurs in the 3-attack offense when the setter is in the left back (LB) position. It often becomes extremely difficult for the setter to get from the left back (LB) position of the court to the setter's position at the net without interfering with the service reception. It also represents a much greater distance to travel than the other two situations (Figure 7.16a_2 and c_2). Two alterantive serve reception patterns are suggested in Figures 9.6a and b. (Use Figure 7.16 for comparison.)

As illustrated in Figure 9.6a, the left front (T$_5$) and left back (S$_6$) players have moved up to the net. This is called the "stagger" or partial W-formation. From his or her position close to the net, the setter can move to the setting position easily and quickly. Figure 9.6b illustrates the "cup" formation. This formation is very similar to the "stagger" formation, with the exception of the placement of the middle front (MB$_4$) player.

Designated Plays

Illustrated in Figure 7.14 are four basic play sets. When these sets are combined, they are referred to as designated plays. The multiple offense is a sophisticated 3-attack offense which is based on

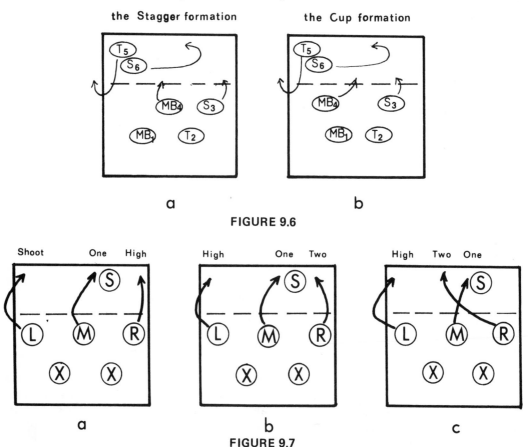

the Stagger formation   the Cup formation

a   b

FIGURE 9.6

Shoot   One   High   High   One   Two   High   Two   One

a   b   c

FIGURE 9.7

designated plays. In essence, each play combination has an assigned number which the setter signals prior to each serve reception. In this section, three designated plays will be introduced. Each play is based on three kinds of sets: (a) the "1" set, (b) the play set, and (c) the outlet or high set.

The "shoot" play. The "shoot" play is illustrated in Figure 9.7a. The on-hand hitter (L) looks for and attacks a set that is low, to the corner, and fast (the play set). The middle hitter (M) moves to the setter (S) and looks for a ball set 30 to 60 centimeters (1 to 2 ft) above the net (the "1" set). In attacking the "1" set, the spiker must be in the air before the ball is set to him or her. Meanwhile, anticipating a poor service reception, the off-hand hitter (R) is looking for a high outside set (the outlet or safety valve).

The "two" play. The "two" play is illustrated in Figure 9.7b. In this play, the on-hand hitter (L) anticipates the outlet set; the middle hitter (M) attacks the "1" set; and the off-hand hitter (R) looks for a low back set (the play set). As illustrated in Figure 7.21, the back "2" set is set about 2 meters above the net.

The "right cross." The "right cross" is illustrated in Figure 9.7c. In this play, the on-hand hitter (L) anticipates the outlet set; the middle hitter (M) attacks the "1" set; and the off-hand hitter (R) cuts behind the middle attacker (M) to hit a front "2" set (the play set). As with the back "2" set, the front "two" is set about 2 meters above the net.

The 5-1 Offense

The 5-1 offense has become a very popular offense in recent years. In essence, the 5-1 offense is a combination of the 4-2 offense and the 3-attack offense. Instead of using two setters, the 5-1 offense only uses one. When the setter is on the front row, the team plays a 4-2 offense. Conversely, when the setter is on the back row, the team plays a 3-attack offense. The basic strength of the offense is that the best setter is called upon to do all the setting. The weakness is that the team only has two attackers when the setter is on the front row. However, a strong hitting setter can put a lot of stress on an opposing defense by jump setting and occasionally spiking the ball (as a front-row player).

SUGGESTED STUDENTS PROJECTS

1. Adopt the preseason training program as outlined in this chapter. After two weeks of training see if you can meet the stated goals.

2. After completing (or in lieu of) project #1, try each of the five competition season drills. Do one a day for 5 days. Which one did you find the most difficult? Would you exclude any of them? Can you think of better ones? If so, write them down in the margin of your book.

3. Go to a high school or college volleyball match and statistically chart a team's spiking and receiving performance using the Dunphy method. Using the results of your charting, can you determine why the team won or lost? Based on your results, which players would you replace in the next game? Which players would you set more in the next game?

4. Go to another volleyball match and chart team performance for an entire match (2 of 3 or 3 of 5 games) using the accumulative method. Chart spiking, passing, and serving. In addition, chart blocking performance using the error method. Analyze the results. See if you can determine the strong and weak players on the team in terms of the skills charted.

5. After reading the section in this chapter on coaching philosophy, sit down and write your own personal philosophy of coaching. Compare it with other students' and ask challenging questions of one another.

REFERENCES

Dunphy, M. "Scouting the Opposition." *Volleyball Magazine,* No. 8 (1977), 8-10.

NAGWS. *National Association for Girls and Women in Sport Volleyball Rules (1978-79).* Washington, D.C.: AAHPER Publications, 1978.

NFSHSA. *National Federation Edition Volleyball Rules 1978-79.* Elgin, Illinois: National Federation of State High School Associations, 1978.

Scates, A.E. *Winning Volleyball.* 2nd ed. Boston: Allyn and Bacon, Inc., 1976.

USVBA. *United States Volleyball Association Official Guide (1979).* San Francisco: United States Volleyball Association, 1978.

10

Tips for Teaching Volleyball to Children

The material covered thus far was designed for persons ranging from the age of twelve through adulthood. However, volleyball play and instruction should begin with the nine-year old (grade 4). This is not to say that the material in this book is not useful to the nine, ten and eleven-year old; but only that certain adaptations should be made.

THE EQUIPMENT

One of the major adjustments that can be made when teaching volleyball to children is to change the equipment. There is no reason that volleyball equipment cannot be adapted to meet the needs of the participants.

The Net

The first and most important adjustment that should be made is in the height of the net. Based on the jumping ability and stature of boys and girls ages 9 to 11, the net should be set no higher than 1.83 meters (about 6 ft). In fact, based on these same measurements, the height of the volleyball net for boys and girls ages 12 to 14 should be set at approximately 2.13 meters (about 7 ft). However, one caution is in order when the volleyball net is lowered. A lowered net makes serving the volleyball much easier, allowing some of the children with strong overhand serves to serve 9 or 10 points (uncontested) in a row. Since this practice eliminates volleying between teams, encourage the boys and girls to serve underhand or to make their overhand serves high and soft.

Court Dimensions

As it is advisable to lower the net for children, it is also recommended that the volleyball court be made smaller. This is especially true of the length of the court. It is often difficult for six small children to adequately cover an entire regulation-size volleyball court. Serving on a regulation court also presents problems. At the very least, the server should be allowed to move to within 6 meters (about 20 ft) of the net when serving the ball. For example, the court might be shortened by 2 meters and the serving line by 3 meters through the laying down of gymnasium tape.

Number of Students

Regardless of the size of the volleyball court, it is never recommended that more than twelve participants (6 per side) be on the court at one time. The common practice of allowing nine and ten students to play side-by-side on the same side of the net is counter-productive. Little learning can take place if a child only touches the ball once out of every 9 or 10 volleys. Rather, it is suggested that the number of children on a team be reduced to three or four and the dimensions of the court be reduced. For example, with a little imagination a single regulation volleyball court could be divided up into two smaller courts (each 4 X 8 meters). This would allow two games instead of one and twice as much ball handling on a single regulation court.

The Ball

When teaching volleyball to children, it is important that soft, lightweight balls be used. Rubber or plastic balls should not be used because they sting the skin. In addition, balls should not be fully inflated (if a ball calls for six pounds of pressure, put in four). One ball that seems to be ideal for children's use is the Tachikara SV-5W Gold volleyball (see chapter 4). Tachikara also puts out a junior-size volleyball designed for use by children. This volleyball (SV-4S) is 62.9 centimeters (24.75 in.) in circumference, whereas the regulation volleyball varies from 65 to 67 centimeters.

THE SKILLS TO BE TAUGHT

The volleyball skills of serving (underhand), forearm passing, and face passing should be taught to children. The skills of spiking and blocking are optional. The skills of diving and rolling (Japanese roll) are recommended for inclusion in a tumbling unit, but not in the volleyball unit.

The Underhand Serve

The underhand serve must be mastered by children learning to play volleyball. Many of the drills that are described in chapter 5 are applicable for the instruction of children.

The Forearm Pass

The forearm pass is also a skill that can be mastered by children learning the game of volleyball. Most of the drills outlined in chapter 5 for learning the bump are also applicable.

The Face Pass

Of the three major skills to be taught to children (serving, bumping, and setting), the skill of face passing (setting) will be the most difficult. This is because of a general lack of finger and arm strength, which is a good reason to teach volleyball to children. As with serving and forearm passing, most of the drills outlined in chapter 5 for face passing will also be applicable here.

Spiking and Blocking

It is not necessary to teach children the spike and block. As interest in the attack phase of the game develops, however, the children should be encouraged to experiment with these skills even though the details of offense and defense need not be taught. The safety aspects of staying on their own side of the net should be emphasized. In addition, the children should be familiarized with a basic receiving formation (see Figure 5.6).

The Forward Dive and Japanese Roll

If the forward dive and Japanese role were taught to children 9 through 11 years of age, the skills would be mastered by the age of fifteen (entering high school). It is not suggested, however, that these advanced skills be taught in a volleyball class to elementary-age children, but the basis of the skills (without ball) could be taught as part of an instructional unit in tumbling and gymnastics. In teaching these tumbling skills to children, the teacher should point out their application to the game of volleyball. For example, the forward dive is identical to the tumbling technique known as the "Swedish fall." The practicality of this suggestion is underscored by my observation that beginning volleyball players who have gymnastics and tumbling experience learn the dive and roll with remarkable ease.

VOLLEYBALL GAMES FOR CHILDREN

One of the most interesting ways to introduce the game of volleyball to children is through the use of lead-up games. In this section, three games for children are described, but for a more comprehensive review of lead-up games, see Scates (1976).

Mini-Volleyball

Mini-volleyball is like regular volleyball, except that the net is lowered to about 1.83 meters, the court is made smaller (about 5 × 10 m), and only three or four players are on a side. This game is interesting to children since it is easy to play and is competitive (motivating), and each player gets to handle the ball frequently. The only real limitation of the game is playing facilities. When played indoors, the use of badminton courts is recommended. If volleyball is played out-of-doors, numerous semipermanent courts could be set up at little cost to the host organization.

In teaching mini-volleyball, it is important that the children be encouraged to play the game correctly (e.g., use three hits and not catch or lift the ball). Failure to encourage the participants to use appropriate volleyball skills and concepts will cause the game to deteriorate into "picnic" or "jungle" volleyball. This sort of volleyball game is counter-productive to the purposes of mini-volleyball.

In many countries mini-volleyball is played as an official game with specific rules, court dimensions, and net height. Students and teachers interested in the specifics of these rules are referred to Scates, pp. 208-210.

Bounce Volleyball

Bounce volleyball is played much like regular volleyball, except that the ball is allowed to bounce once before it is hit. The server either tosses the ball into play (underhand) or serves underhand. In either case he or she takes as many attempts as necessary to get the ball into play. Serve should be made from within 6 meters (about 20 ft) of the net.

As with mini-volleyball, the children should be encouraged to handle the ball properly, but not penalized if they make illegal hits. They should likewise be encouraged to use all three allowable hits. While the ball may bounce once before it is hit, it is not mandatory that the ball bounce. More than six players per team may play bounce volleyball, but increased individual ball handling will result if six or fewer play.

Keep-It-Up

Keep-it-up is a volleyball lead-up game in which neither team can lose. Play begins with an easy underhand serve as in bounce volleyball. The objective of the game is to volley the ball into the air as many times as possible without it touching the ground. The score is the number of consecutive volleys made by both sides combined. As with regulation volleyball, the ball may not be hit more than three times before it is volleyed across the net to the cooperating "opponents." A score of 20 consecutive hits would be considered fair, while 50 would be excellent. Competition can be inserted into the game by having one court of twelve players compete with an adjacent court of twelve players.

As with mini-volleyball and bounce volleyball, proper ball handling and the use of all three allowable hits should be encouraged but not enforced.

GERONTOLOGICAL CONSIDERATIONS

Volleyball is a game that can be played by people of all ages. The materials in this book, and specifically this chapter, may be adapted for use by the elderly. As society begins to pay more attention to the needs of the elderly, more elderly people will become involved in the learning of new recreational skills. Teaching volleyball (as a new skill) to the elderly should be approached much the same way as outlined in this chapter for teaching children. The elderly person who is a beginner in volleyball may find this approach stimulating.

SUGGESTED STUDENT PROJECTS

1. Three lead-up games have been suggested in this chapter. Without referring to any resource material, create one additional lead-up game. Give the game a name and specify the rules.

2. After gaining approval from the school principal and physical education teacher in your city, visit an elementary school and observe the manner in which volleyball is being taught to children. What suggestions for improvement could you make? What practices are used by the teacher that you think are especially useful?

REFERENCE

Scates, A.E. *Winning Volleyball.* 2nd ed. Boston: Allyn and Bacon, Inc., 1976.

Bibliography of Books, Films, and Periodicals

BOOKS

AAHPER. *Volleyball Skills Test Manual* (Boys and Girls). Washington, D.C.: AAHPER Publications, 1969. 36 pages.

Boyden, E.D., and R. Burton. *Staging Successful Tournaments.* New York: Association Press, 1957. 171 pages.

Bratton, R.D. *300 Plus Volleyball Drills and Ideas.* Ottawa, Ontario: Canadian Volleyball Association, 1975. 170 pages.

Brumbach, W.B.; C.M. McGown; and B.A. Borrevik. *Beginning Volleyball: A Syllabus for Teachers.* Rev. ed. Eugene: University of Oregon Press, 1972. 69 pages.

Cherebetiu, G. *Volleyball Techniques.* Hollywood, California: Creative Book Co., 1968. 140 pages.

Cohen, H. *Power Volleyball Drills.* Hollywood, California: Creative Sports Books, 1967.

Coleman, J., and T. Liskevych. *Pictorial Analysis of Power Volleyball.* Hollywood, California: Creative Book Co., 1968. 146 pages.

CVA. *International Federation Coaches Manual.* Ottawa, Ontario: Canadian Volleyball Association, 1975. 242 pages.

Egstrom, G.H., and F. Schaafsma. *Volleyball.* 2nd ed. Dubuque, Iowa: Wm. C. Brown Co., 1972. 58 pages.

Hartman, P.E. *Volleyball Fundamentals.* Columbus, Ohio: C.E. Merrill Publishing Co., 1968. 68 pages.

Herzog, K. *Volleyball Movements in Photographic Sequence.* Ottawa, Ontario: Canadian Volleyball Association, 1976. (Address: Volleyball Publications, 333 River Road, Vanier City, Ontario, KIL 8B9).

Keller, V. *Point, Game and Match!* Hollywood, California: Creative Book Co., 1968. 98 pages.

Keller, V. *Coaching Supplement to Point, Game and Match.* San Francisco, California: United States Volleyball Association, 1971. 72 pages.

Keller, V. *National Coaches Technical Module.* Huntington Beach, California: United States Volleyball Association, 1977.

Laveaga, R. *Volleyball.* 2nd ed. New York: Ronald Press, 1960. 128 pages.

Nicholls, K. *Modern Volleyball.* London: Henry Kimpton Publishers, 1973. 281 pages.

Odeneal, W.T.; H.E. Wilson; and M.F. Kellam. *Beginning Volleyball.* Rev. ed. Belmont, California: Wadsworth Publishing Co., 1969. 35 pages.

Peck, W. *Volleyball*. New York: Macmillan Publishing Co. 1969. 128 pages.

Peppler, M.S. *Inside Volleyball for Women*. Chicago: Contemporary Books, Inc., 1977. 90 pages.

Robinson, B. *Sports Illustrated Volleyball*. Philadelphia: J.B. Lippincott Co., 1972. 90 pages.

Sandefur, R. *Volleyball*. Pacific Palisades, California: Goodyear Publishing Company, 1970. 80 pages.

Scates, A.B. *Winning Volleyball*. 2nd ed. Boston: Allyn and Bacon, 1976. 295 pages.

Scates, A.B., and J. Ward. *Concepts and Skills of Volleyball*. 2nd ed. Boston: Allyn and Bacon, 1975. 96 pages.

Schaafsma, F., and A. Heck. *Volleyball for Coaches and Teachers*. Dubuque, Iowa: Wm. C. Brown Co., 1971. 64 pages.

Schurman, D. *Volleyball: A Guide to Skills and Strategy*. New York: Antheneum Publishers, 1976. 141 pages.

Shondell, D., and J.I. McManama. *Volleyball*. Englewood Cliffs, New Jersey: Prentice-Hall Inc., 1971. 99 pages.

Slaymaker, T., and V. Brown. *Power Volleyball*. 2nd ed. Philadelphia: W.B. Saunders Company, 1976. 115 pages.

Tennant, M. *Volleyball Team Play*. Ottawa, Ontario: Canadian Volleyball Association, 1977. 132 pages.

Thigpen, J. *Power Volleyball for Girls and Women*. Dubuque, Iowa: Wm. C. Brown Co., 1974. 134 pages.

Trotter, B.J. *Volleyball for Girls and Women*. New York: Ronald Press, 1965. 227 pages.

Welch, J.E. *How to Play and Teach Volleyball*. Rev. ed. New York: Association Press, 1969. 192 pages.

PERIODICALS

Volleyball Review—Official Publication of the USVBA. USVBA Publication, P.O. Box 77065, San Francisco, California 94107.

The *Volleyball Review* is the official periodical of the United States Volleyball Association, and is distributed four times a year at irregular intervals. The major purpose of the publication is to inform USVBA members of the status of volleyball in the United States and the progress of U.S. International teams.

Volleyball Magazine. P.O. Box 2410, Boulder, Colorado 80321.

Volleyball Magazine is a quality periodical that is distributed at regular intervals six times a year. It regularly contains excellent volleyball action photos; features on indoor USVBA competition; articles on professional volleyball; sand volleyball; short stories; indepth interviews with volleyball personalities; and a very useful "Technique Handbook" section. From the point of view of the teacher and coach, the "Technique Handbook" sections are extremely useful. Each section deals with a specific volleyball topic and is written by a current expert on the subject.

FILMS

For Purchase

Power Volleyball. Instructional Film-Loop Series. Members of the gold-medal-winning men's and women's U.S. Pan American Games volleyball teams demonstrate the latest techniques used by volleyball teams around the world. Most players are former All-Americans with experience in national championship competition and in international tournaments. Super 8-mm or standard 8-mm films sell for $19.95 each. Set of five sells for $95.00. For purchase, write:

The Athletic Institute
200 N. Castlewood Drive
North Palm Beach, Florida 33408

Volleyball. Instructional Film-Loop Series. Experts in the game of volleyball illustrate proper execution of the basic skills. Set of six film books. Purchase price is $144.00 per set. For purchase, write:

BFA Educational Media
2211 Michigan Avenue
Santa Monica, California 90404

Volleyball. Instructional Film-Loop Series. Larry Rundle, Toshi Toyoda, and outstanding college players demonstrate the basic skills of volleyball. Authored by UCLA coach, Al Scates, and produced by the Ealing Corporation in cooperation with NCAA/AAHPER. Super 8 mm, silent, 3.5 minutes each, color. Sells for $24.95 each of $149.70 for a 6-loop set. For purchase, write:

NCAA Films
P.O. Box 2726
Wichita, Kansas 67201

Volleyball U.S.A. Origin of the sport is traced. Fundamentals and basic skills are emphasized through the use of slow-motion and stop-action photography. Exhibition of how the game can be played is excitingly portrayed through highlights of a national championship. 17 minutes, 16 mm, sound, black and white. Purchase price is $95.00. For purchase, write:

Association Instructional Materials
600 Madison Avenue
New York, New York 10022

Women's Power Volleyball. Members of the E Pluribus Unum 1973 AAU and USVBA National Women's Volleyball Tournament demonstrate the proper execution of seven basic skills in volleyball. Each skill (or skill combination) is self-contained as a Super 8-mm color loop film cartridge. Each cartridge lasts approximately 3.5 minutes and sells for $24.95. For purchase, write:

The Athletic Institute
200 N. Castlewood Drive
North Palm Beach, Florida 33408

For Rental

Japanese Training Film. Japanese National Men's Team. Japanese players demonstrate nearly perfect technique on the basic skills in volleyball. Men's training program is highlighted. 35 minutes, color, 16 mm. Rental fee is $50.00. May be rented from:

C. R. Ignacio
P.O. Box 4731
Carson, California 90745

The Olympic Finals (1976). Filmed highlights of the men's and women's 1976 Olympic finals (Poland vs. USSR and Japan vs. USSR). Color, Super 8 mm, sound. Each film (match) rents for $25.00 per week. May be rented from:

> USVBA Film Library
> Graceland College
> Lamoni, Iowa 50140

Play Volleyball. Uses a team of experienced men players to demonstrate the skills of serving, receiving, passing, setting, and blocking in volleyball. Stop-action and slow-motion photography are used to clarify the essentials of each of these skills. 16 mm, black and white, 20 minutes. Rental fee is $3.60. May be rented from:

> Visual Aids Service
> University of Illinois
> Division of University Extension
> Champaign, Illinois 61820

USVBA Championships. Filmed highlights of the men's and women's 1977 USVBA National Championships (Chucks vs. Maccabi and Spoilers vs. Adidas); and the 1978 USVBA Championships (Chucks vs. Outrigger and Nick's vs. King Harbor Spoilers). Color, Super 8 mm, sound. Each film (match) rents for $25.00 per week. May be rented from:

> USVBA Film Library
> Graceland College
> Lamoni, Iowa 50140

Volleyball for Boys. An actual high school volleyball team provides an in-depth study of individual and team skills, emphasizing serving, passing, setting, and spiking. 16 mm, color (2nd ed.), 14 minutes. Rental fee is $10.00. May be rented from:

> University of Kansas Film Service
> 746 Massachusetts Street
> Lawrence, Kansas 66044
> or
> Central Arizona Film Cooperative
> Arizona State University
> Tempe, Arizona 85281

Volleyball Techniques for Girls. Shows a variety of basic playing skills. Uses animation and slow motion to analyze the basic techniques involved in the overhand volley, spiking, underhand volley, blocking, serving. 16 mm, black and white, 12 minutes. Rental fee is $6.60. May be rented from:

> Educational Media Center
> Stadium Building
> University of Colorado
> Boulder, Colorado 80309

Volleyball–Dig It. Kathy Gregory, member of the U.S. Olympic team, discusses the skills of volleyball as they are demonstrated by some of the best women volleyball players in the United States.

Each skill is examined precisely, with particular emphasis placed upon the importance of timing. 16 mm, color, 14 minutes. Rental fee is $10.00. May be rented from:

> University of Kansas Film Service
> 746 Massachusetts Street
> Lawrence, Kansas 66044

Volleyball Drills and Techniques. Championship men players demonstrate elementary and advanced drills for volleyball. Analyzes the most important techniques for each of thirty drills and shows methods used in demonstrating skills. 16 mm, black and white, 16 minutes. Rental fee is $3.40. May be rented from:

> Visual Aids Service
> University of Illinois
> Division of University Extension
> Champaign, Illinois 61820

Volleyball Skills. Analyzes and demonstrates correct fundamental techniques of volleyball. Covers serving, receiving, setting, spiking, and blocking. Shown in regular and slow motion using championship players. 16 mm, black and white, 13 minutes. Rental fee is $7.50. May be rented from:

> Educational Media Center
> 207 Milton Bennion Hall
> University of Utah
> Salt Lake City, Utah 84112

Volleyball—Skills and Practices. Uses normal and slow motion to show six specific volleyball skills and to explain the proper techniques to perfect each skill. 16 mm, color, 12 minutes. Rental fee is $5.35. May be rented from:

> Audiovisual Center
> Oklahoma State University
> Stillwater, Oklahoma 74074

Volleyball USA. Origin of the sport is traced. Fundamentals and basic skills are emphasized through the use of slow-motion and stop-action photography. Exhibition of how the game can be played is excitingly portrayed through highlights of a national championship. 16 mm, black and white, sound, 17 minutes. Rental fee is $6.00 per day. May be rented from:

> Association Instructional Materials
> 600 Madison Avenue
> New York, New York 10022

Volleyball for Women. Outstanding women players demonstrate elementary and advanced skills of volleyball in regular-speed and slow-motion scenes. Includes game play, fundamentals, drills for learning skills, and team strategy. 16 mm, black and white, 16 minutes. Rental fee is $3.70. May be rented from:

> Visual Aids Service
> University of Illinois
> Division of University Extension
> Champaign, Illinois 61820

Index